George D. Mackay

**The earthly footprints of our risen Lord illumined:**

A continuous narrative of the four Gospels according to the Revised version

George D. Mackay

**The earthly footprints of our risen Lord illumined:**
*A continuous narrative of the four Gospels according to the Revised version*

ISBN/EAN: 9783337714512

Printed in Europe, USA, Canada, Australia, Japan

Cover: Foto ©ninafisch / pixelio.de

More available books at **www.hansebooks.com**

# THE

# EARTHLY FOOTPRINTS

OF OUR

# RISEN LORD.

## Illumined.

A CONTINUOUS NARRATIVE OF THE FOUR GOSPELS
ACCORDING TO THE REVISED VERSION.

WITH AN INTRODUCTION BY

## REV. JOHN HALL, D.D.

FLEMING H. REVELL COMPANY.

NEW YORK: | CHICAGO:
30 Union Square: East. | 148-150 Madison Street.

*Publishers of Evangelical Literature.*

The Carton Press

171, 173 Macdougal Street, New York

# COMPILER'S PREFACE.

WE know from blessed experience that many dear people looking, at first. only with curious eyes at the *pictured* incidents of the life of the Lord Jesus Christ upon the earth, have afterwards come to gaze with tearful eyes at the same—their hearts the while full of joy—they having become assured of the forgiveness of their sins, and of having received the gift of eternal life.

This knowledge, gained during the last two years in our efforts to bring men, women and children to the loving Saviour by appealing to their hearts through their sense of sight as well as through their sense of hearing, led us to think and conclude that a judicious selection from the pictures thus presented—say, one hundred of them suitably reproduced—would effectively serve the sacred purpose of illustrating a new life of our Lord,—to be compiled from the *revised* version of the writings of the four evangelists.

In this way, we thought, an appeal to the heart through

the eye, could be made far beyond our own or anybody's personal superintendence—even to the remotest parts of our land—if God should be pleased to prosper the enterprise.

With the assistance of a Christian brother we have now completed a work so projected; its distinctive features being,

First — *The Illustrations.*

Second—The fact that the reading-matter has been compiled entirely from the writings of the four evangelists *according to the Revised Version.*

Third—The additional fact that in deference to the as yet prevailing prejudice against the paragraphic form of the composition of the Revised Version, verses distinct and separate have been made of the matter gathered therefrom; so that the pages of the new book should resemble the more familiar pages of the *unrevised* version of the same blessed truths.

And now we send the book forth, such as it is, praying God to make it to many a re-enjoyment of the " Stereopticon Illustrated Readings of the Life of Jesus;"

To many, a delightful reminder of the blessed hour when the very words and pictures on the pages before them influenced them, in some degree at least, to give their hearts and devote their lives to God;

And especially beseeching Him that by His providence it may fall into the hands of some who looked with curious eyes only, and went their way with their hearts unaffected; and that He may lead such to a perusal of the sacred story with its illustrations in the quiet of their own homes; and so, after all, His spirit moving their hearts and minds, they be brought to true repentance and into that peace which passeth all understanding.

And as Christ said to his disciples, "Ask what ye will," we pray God that through the effort we have made in this way to serve the blessed Master, multitudes even may find the only real happiness possible in this world of sin and sorrow, and finally enter into the everlasting joy of the Christian's world to come.

The illustrations consist of original drawings by C. P. Davis, E. J. Whitney, and August Wills, and copies of pictures by Bida, Heck, Hofman, Hunt, Munkacsy, Müller, Plockhurst, Raphael, Paul Veronese, De Vinci, and other masters in sacred art.

GEORGE D. MACKAY.

NEW YORK.

# INTRODUCTION.

A FTER looking carefully into the plan and the pages of this book, fittingly called THE EARTHLY FOOT-PRINTS OF OUR RISEN LORD, I am happy to commend it, for reasons, among others, like the following.

One of the evidences of Divine wisdom in the structure of the Bible is the extent to which its teaching is presented in history. Facts are noticed and remembered more easily than abstract statements. The historic facts of the inspired records stand out as object-lessons for all lands and for all times.

On the same principle it is that persons readily arrest attention, and gain a place in the thought of observer and of reader. With what distinctness do the men and women of holy Scripture stand out before us! It is not to be wondered at that preachers and teachers have so frequently and effectively grouped the great truths they meant to enforce around " Scripture Characters."

# INTRODUCTION.

These statements are emphatically true of the Gospels—that portion of the written word in which the " Word made flesh" is presented to men from several distinct points of view. He in His grace and loveliness, stands forth, the Central figure, giving interest and significance to the persons coming around Him, whether as disciples or as enemies, and suggesting pictures which the mind cannot but try to shape for itself. We think of the "holy child Jesus," the home in which He lived, the boat on the lake in which He was so often carried, the garden trees under which He prayed, the cross on which He gave His life, the grave from which He came forth. To render these memory-pictures distinct and definite, is an important contribution to Christian intelligence. This contribution the compiler has made.

Nor are we to overlook the fact that travel, Oriental research and the study of ancient monuments—so many of which corroborate Bible history—make it easier than it once was, to secure illustrations that will be true to the truth of things. The dress, the homes, the furniture, the surroundings of the Orientals two thousand years ago, are now matters of definite knowledge, and of comparatively easy reproduction. One can see the results in such works as Smith's "Dictionary of the Bible," or in a good modern encyclopædia. Here they are made to throw light upon a life, like which the world never saw another.

## INTRODUCTION.

The effort to utilize this method of giving interest and distinctness to Scripture scenes and incidents will, we doubt not, be successful with many, both young and old, and will extend and deepen the knowledge of Gospel history. Pictures have been turned into helps to prayer till they became, all too often, the objects of devotional regard; but this has been by those who had not the Divine word in their hands. Illustrations, such as are here presented, draw to the reading and knowledge of the Word, and the Word folds "God as a spirit," and teaches men to "worship Him in spirit and in truth," and for fitting and needed help to seek the Spirit of grace and of supplications. A preacher labors to fix human attention on Christ Jesus. This work will be a help in this high, this divinely-appointed labor.

*John Hall*

NEW YORK.

# THE EARTHLY FOOTPRINTS

OF

## OUR RISEN LORD.

### 𝕴𝖑𝖑𝖚𝖒𝖎𝖓𝖊𝖉.

---

## CHAPTER I.

### THE PROLOGUE.

IN the beginning was the Word, and the Word was with God, and the Word was God.

2 The same was in the beginning with God.

3 All things were made by him; and without him was not anything made that hath been made.

4 In him was life; and the life was the light of men.

5 And the light shineth in the darkness; and the darkness apprehended it not.

6 There came a man, sent from God, whose name was John.

7 The same came for witness, that he might bear witness of the light, that all might believe through him.

8 He was not the light, but *came* that he might bear witness of the light.

9 There was the true light, *even the light* which lighteth every man, coming into the world.

10 He was in the world, and the world was made by him, and the world knew him not.

11 He came unto his own, and they that were his own received him not.

12 But as many as received him, to them gave he the right to become children of

God, *even* to them that believe on his name:

13 Which were born, not of blood, nor of the will of the flesh, nor of the will of man, but of God.

14 And the Word became flesh, and dwelt among us (and we beheld his glory, glory as of the only begotten from the Father), full of grace and truth.

15 John beareth witness of him, and crieth, saying, This was he of whom I said, He that cometh after me is become before me: for he was before me.

16 For of his fulness we all received, and grace for grace.

17 For the law was given by Moses; grace and truth came by Jesus Christ.

18 No man hath seen God at any time; the only begotten Son, which is in the bosom of the Father, he hath declared *him*.

THE BAPTIST FORETOLD.

October, B. C. 6.

19 THERE was in the days of Herod, king of Judæa, a certain priest named Zacharias, of the course of Abijah: and he had a wife of the daughters of Aaron, and her name was Elisabeth.

20 And they were both righteous before God, walking in all the commandments and ordinances of the Lord blameless.

21 And they had no child, because that Elisabeth was barren, and they both were *now* well stricken in years.

22 Now it came to pass, while he executed the priest's office before God in the order of his course,

23 According to the custom of the priest's office, his lot was to enter into the temple of the Lord and burn incense.

24 And the whole multitude of the people were praying without at the hour of incense.

25 And there appeared unto him an angel of the Lord standing on the right side of the altar of incense.

26 And Zacharias was

ZACHARIAS AND THE ANGEL.

troubled when he saw *him*, and fear fell upon him.

27 But the angel said unto him, Fear not, Zacharias: because thy supplication is heard, and thy wife Elisabeth shall bear thee a son, and thou shalt call his name John.

28 And thou shalt have joy and gladness; and many shall rejoice at his birth.

29 For he shall be great in the sight of the Lord, and he shall drink no wine nor strong drink; and he shall be filled with the Holy Ghost, even from his mother's womb.

30 And many of the children of Israel shall he turn unto the Lord their God.

31 And he shall go before his face in the spirit and power of Elijah, to turn the hearts of the fathers to the children, and the disobedient *to walk* in the wisdom of the just; to make ready for the Lord a people prepared *for him*.

32 And Zacharias said unto the angel, Whereby shall I know this? for I am an old man, and my wife well stricken in years.

33 And the angel answering said unto him, I am Gabriel, that stand in the presence of God; and I was sent to speak unto thee, and to bring thee these good tidings.

34 And behold, thou shalt be silent and not able to speak, until the day that these things shall come to pass, because thou believedst not my words, which shall be fulfilled in their season.

35 And the people were waiting for Zacharias, and they marvelled while he tarried in the temple.

36 And when he came out he could not speak unto them: and they perceived that he had seen a vision in the temple: and he continued making signs unto them, and remained dumb.

37 And it came to pass, when the days of his minis-

tration were fulfilled, he departed unto his house.

38 And after these days Elisabeth his wife conceived; and she hid herself five months, saying,

39 Thus hath the Lord done unto me in the days wherein he looked upon *me*, to take away my reproach among men.

## CHAPTER II.
### THE ANNUNCIATION.
#### March, B. C. 5.

NOW in the sixth month the angel Gabriel was sent from God unto a city of Galilee, named Nazareth,

2 To a virgin betrothed to a man whose name was Joseph, of the house of David ; and the virgin's name was Mary.

3 And he came in unto her, and said, Hail, thou that art highly favoured, the Lord *is* with thee.

4 But she was greatly troubled at the saying, and cast in her mind what manner of salutation this might be.

5 And the angel said unto her, Fear not, Mary: for thou hast found favour with God.

6 And behold, thou shalt conceive in thy womb, and bring forth a son, and shall call his name JESUS.

7 He shall be great, and shall be called the Son of the Most High: and the Lord God shall give unto him the throne of his father David:

8 And he shall reign over the house of Jacob for ever; and of his kingdom there shall be no end.

9 And Mary said unto the angel, How shall this be, seeing I know not a man ?

10 And the angel answered and said unto her, The Holy Ghost shall come upon thee, and the power of the Most High shall overshadow thee: wherefore also that which is to be born shall be called holy, the Son of God.

11 And behold, Elisabeth thy kinswoman, she also hath conceived a son in her old age: and this is the

THE ANGEL GABRIEL APPEARS TO MARY.

sixth month with her that was called barren.

12 For no word from God shall be void of power.

13 And Mary said, Behold, the handmaid of the Lord; be it unto me according to thy word. And the angel departed from her.

14 And Mary arose in these days and went into the hill country with haste, into a city of Judah;

15 And entered into the house of Zacharias and saluted Elisabeth.

16 And it came to pass, when Elisabeth heard the salutation of Mary, the babe leaped in her womb; and Elisabeth was filled with the Holy Ghost;

17 And she lifted up her voice with a loud cry, and said, Blessed *art* thou among women, and blessed *is* the fruit of thy womb.

18 And whence is this to me, that the mother of my Lord should come unto me?

19 For behold, when the voice of thy salutation came into mine ears, the babe leaped in my womb for joy.

20 And blessed *is* she that believed; for there shall be a fulfilment of the things which have been spoken to her from the Lord.

21 And Mary said,

My soul doth magnify the Lord,

22 And my spirit hath rejoiced in God my Saviour.

23 For he hath looked upon the low estate of his handmaiden:

For behold, from henceforth all generations shall call me blessed.

24 For he that is mighty hath done to me great things;

And holy is his name.

25 And his mercy is unto generations and generations.

On them that fear him.

26 He hath showed strength with his arm;

He ' hath scattered the proud in the imagination of their heart.

27 He hath put down princes from *their* thrones,

And hath exalted them of low degree.

28 The hungry he hath filled with good things;

And the rich he hath sent empty away.

29 He hath holpen Israel his servant,

That he might remember mercy

30 (As he spake unto our fathers)

Toward Abraham and his seed for ever.

31 And Mary abode with her about three months, and returned unto her house.

## CHAPTER III.
### THE BAPTIST BORN.
#### June, b. c. 5.

NOW Elisabeth's time was fulfilled that she should be delivered; and she brought forth a son.

32 And her neighbours and her kinsfolk heard that the Lord had magnified his mercy towards her; and they rejoiced with her.

3 And it came to pass on the eighth day, that they came to circumcise the child; and they would have called him Zacharias, after the name of his father.

4 And his mother answered and said, Not so; but he shall be called John.

5 And they said unto her, There is none of thy kindred that is called by this name.

6 And they made signs to his father, what he would have him called.

7 And he asked for a writing tablet, and wrote, saying, His name is John.

8 And they marvelled all. And his mouth was opened immediately, and his tongue *loosed*, and he spake, blessing God.

9 And fear came on all that dwelt round about them:

10 And all these sayings were noised abroad throughout all the hill country of Judæa.

11 And all that heard them laid them up in their

MARY AT THE HOME OF ELIZABETH.

heart, saying, What then shall this child be? For the hand of the Lord was with him.

12 And his father Zacharias was filled with the Holy Ghost, and prophesied, saying,

13 Blessed *be* the Lord, the God of Israel;

For he hath visited and wrought redemption for his people,

14 And hath raised up a horn of salvation for us

In the house of his servant David

15 (As he spake by the mouth of his holy prophets which have been since the world began),

16 Salvation from our enemies, and from the hand of all that hate us:

17 To shew mercy towards our fathers,

And to remember his holy covenant;

18 The oath which he sware unto Abraham our father,

19 To grant unto us that we being delivered out of the hand of our enemies

Should serve him without fear,

20 In holiness and righteousness before him all our days.

21 Yea and thou, child, shall be called the prophet of the Most High:

For thou shalt go before the face of the Lord to make ready his ways;

22 To give knowledge of salvation unto his people

In the remission of their sins,

23 Because of the tender mercy of our God,

Whereby the dayspring from on high shall visit us,

24 To shine upon them that sit in darkness and the shadow of death;

To guide our feet into the way of peace.

25 And the child grew, and waxed strong in spirit, and was in the deserts till the day of his shewing unto Israel.

## CHAPTER IV.

### THE BIRTH OF JESUS.

NOW the birth of Jesus Christ was on this wise: When his mother Mary had been betrothed to Joseph, before they came together she was found with child of the Holy Ghost.

2 And Joseph her husband, being a righteous man, and not willing to make her a public example, was minded to put her away privily.

3 But when he thought on these things, behold, an angel of the Lord appeared unto him in a dream; saying, Joseph, thou son of David, fear not to take unto thee Mary thy wife: for that which is conceived in her is of the Holy Ghost.

4 And she shall bring forth a son; and thou shalt call his name JESUS; for it is he that shall save his people from their sins.

5 Now all this is come to pass, that it might be ful- filled which was spoken by the Lord through the prophet, saying,

6 Behold, the virgin shall be with child, and shall bring forth a son,

And they shall call his name Immanuel;

Which is, being interpreted, God with us.

7 And Joseph arose from his sleep, and did as the angel of the Lord commanded him, and took unto him his wife;

8 And knew her not till she had brought forth a son: and he called his name JESUS.

9 Now it came to pass in those days, there went out a decree from Cæsar Augustus, that all the world should be enrolled.

10 This was the first enrolment made when Quirinius was governor of Syria.

11 And all went to enrol themselves, every one to his own city.

12 And Joseph also went up from Galilee, out of the

THE SHEPHERDS SEE THE ANGEL OF THE LORD.

city of Nazareth, into Judæa, to the city of David,
which is called Bethlehem,
because he was of the house
and family of David;

13 To enrol himself with
Mary, who was betrothed to
him, being great with child.

14 And it came to pass,
while they were there, the
days were fulfilled that she
should be delivered.

December, B. C. 5.

15 And she brought forth
her first-born son; and she
wrapped him in swaddling
clothes, and laid him in a
manger, because there was
no room for them in the
inn.

16 And there were shep-
herds in the same country
abiding in the field, and
keeping watch by night over
their flock.

17 And an angel of the
Lord stood by them, and the
glory of the Lord shone
round about them: and they
were sore afraid.

18 And the angel said
unto them, Be not afraid;

for behold, I bring you good
tidings of great joy which
shall be to all the people:

19 For there is born to
you this day in the city of
David a Saviour, which is
Christ the Lord.

20 And this *is* the sign
unto you; Ye shall find a
babe wrapped in swaddling
clothes, and lying in a
manger.

21 And suddenly there
was with the angel a multitude of the heavenly host
praising God, and saying,

Glory to God in the
highest,

22 And on earth peace
among men in whom he is
well pleased.

23 And it came to pass,
when the angels went away
from them into heaven, the
shepherds said one to an-
other, Let us now go even
unto Bethlehem, and see this
thing that is come to pass,
which the Lord hath made
known unto us.

24 And they came with
haste, and found both Mary

and Joseph, and the babe lying in the manger.

25 And when they saw it, they made known concerning the saying which was spoken to them about this child.

26 And all that heard it wondered at the things which were spoken unto them by the shepherds.

27 But Mary kept all these sayings, pondering them in her heart.

28 And the shepherds returned, glorifying and praising God for all the things that they had heard and seen, even as it was spoken unto them.

29 And when eight days were fulfilled for circumcising him, his name was called JESUS, which was so called by the angel before he was conceived in the womb.

30 And when the days of their purification according to the law of Moses were fulfilled, they brought him up to Jerusalem, to present him to the Lord

31 (As it is written in the law of the Lord, Every male that openeth the womb shall be called holy to the Lord),

32 And to offer a sacrifice according to that which is said in the law of the Lord, A pair of turtledoves, or two young pigeons.

33 And behold, there was a man in Jerusalem, whose name was Simeon; and this man was righteous and devout, looking for the consolation of Israel: and the Holy Spirit was upon him.

34 And it had been revealed unto him by the Holy Spirit, that he should not see death, before he had seen the Lord's Christ.

35 And he came in the Spirit into the temple: and when the parents brought in the child Jesus, that they might do concerning him after the custom of the law,

36 Then he received him into his arms, and blessed God, and said,

37 Now lettest thou thy servant depart, O Lord,

MARY AND THE TURTLE DOVES.

According to thy word, in peace:

38 For mine eyes have seen thy salvation,

39 Which thou hast prepared before the face of all peoples;

40 A light for revelation to the Gentiles,

And the glory of thy people Israel.

41 And his father and his mother were marvelling at the things which were spoken concerning him;

42 And Simeon blessed them, and said unto Mary his mother, Behold, this *child* is set for the falling and rising up of many in Israel; and for a sign which is spoken against;

43 Yea, and a sword shall pierce through thine own soul; that thoughts out of many hearts may be revealed.

44 And there was one Anna, a prophetess, the daughter of Phanuel, of the tribe of Asher (she was of a great age, having lived with a husband seven years from her virginity,

45 And she had been a widow even for fourscore and four years), which departed not from the temple, worshipping with fastings and supplications night and day.

46 And coming up at that very hour she gave thanks unto God, and spake of him to all them that were looking for the redemption of Jerusalem.

## CHAPTER V.

February, B. C. 4.

NOW when Jesus was born in Bethlehem of Judæa in the days of Herod the king, behold, wise men from the east came to Jerusalem, saying,

2 Where is he that is born King of the Jews? for we saw his star in the east, and are come to worship him.

3 And when Herod the king heard it, he was troubled, and all Jerusalem with him.

4 And gathering together all the chief priests and scribes of the people, he inquired of them where the Christ should be born.

5 And they said unto him, In Bethlehem of Judæa: for thus it is written by the prophet,

6 And thou Bethlehem, land of Judah,

Art in no wise least among the princes of Judah:

For out of thee shall come forth a governor,

Which shall be shepherd of my people Israel.

7 Then Herod privily called the wise men, and learned of them carefully what time the star appeared.

8 And he sent them to Bethlehem, and said, Go and search out carefully concerning the young child; and when ye have found *him*, bring me word, that I also may come and worship him.

9 And they, having heard the king, went their way; and lo, the star, which they saw in the east, went before them, till it came and stood over where the young child was.

10 And when they saw the star they rejoiced with exceeding great joy.

11 And they came into the house and saw the young child with Mary his mother; and they fell down and worshipped him; and opening their treasures they offered unto him gifts, gold and frankincense and myrrh.

12 And being warned *of God* in a dream that they should not return to Herod, they departed into their own country another way.

13 Now when they were departed, behold, an angel of the Lord appeareth to Joseph in a dream, saying, Arise and take the young child and his mother, and flee into Egypt, and be thou there until I tell thee: for Herod will seek the young child to destroy him.

March, B. C. 4.

14 And he arose and took

THE WISE MEN BRINGING THEIR GIFTS TO JESUS.

the young child and his mother by night, and departed into Egypt;

15 And was there until the death of Herod: that it might be fulfilled which was spoken by the Lord through the prophet, saying, Out of Egypt did I call my son.

16 Then Herod, when he saw that he was mocked of the wise men, was exceeding wroth, and sent forth, and slew all the male children that were in Bethlehem, and in all the borders thereof, from two years old and under, according to the time which he had carefully learned of the wise men.

17 Then was fulfilled that which was spoken by Jeremiah the prophet, saying,

18 A voice was heard in Ramah,

Weeping and great mourning,

Rachel weeping for her children;

And she would not be comforted, because they are not.

19 But when Herod was dead, behold, an angel of the Lord appeareth in a dream to Joseph in Egypt, saying,

20 Arise and take the young child and his mother, and go into the land of Israel: for they are dead that sought the young child's life.

21 And he arose and took the young child and his mother, and came into the land of Israel.

22 But when he heard that Archelaus was reigning over Judæa in the room of his father Herod, he was afraid to go thither; and being warned *of God* in a dream, he withdrew into the parts of Galilee,

23 And came and dwelt in a city called Nazareth: that it might be fulfilled which was spoken by the prophets, that he should be called a Nazarene.

·THE BOY JESUS.

A D. 8 -26.

24 And the child grew,

and waxed strong, filled with wisdom: and the grace of God was upon him.

25 Now his parents went every year to Jerusalem at the feast of the passover.

26 And when he was twelve years old, they went up after the custom of the feast;

27 And when they had fulfilled the days, as they were returning, the boy Jesus tarried behind in Jerusalem; and his parents knew it not;

28 But supposing him to be in the company, they went a day's journey; and they sought for him among their kinsfolk and acquaintance:

29 And when they found him not, they returned to Jerusalem, seeking for him.

30 And it came to pass, after three days they found him in the temple, sitting in the midst of the doctors, both hearing them, and asking them questions:

31 And all that heard him were amazed at his understanding and his answers.

32 And when they saw him, they were astonished: and his mother said unto him, Son, why hast thou thus dealt with us? behold, thy father and I sought thee sorrowing.

33 And he said unto them, How is it that ye sought me? wist ye not that I must be in my Father's house?

34 And they understood not the saying which he spake unto them.

35 And he went down with them, and came to Nazareth; and he was subject unto them: and his mother kept all *these* sayings in her heart.

36 And Jesus advanced in wisdom and stature, and in favour with God and men.

## CHAPTER VI.

### THE PREACHING OF JOHN.

#### A D. 27.

NOW in the fifteenth year of the reign of Tiberius Cæsar, Pontius Pilate being

JESUS IN THE TEMPLE.

governor of Judæa, and Herod being tetrarch of Galilee, and his brother Philip tetrarch of the region of Ituræa and Trachonitis, and Lysanias tetrarch of Abilene,

2 In the high-priesthood of Annas and Caiaphas, the word of God came unto John the son of Zacharias in the wilderness.

3 And he came into all the region round about Jordan, preaching the baptism of repentance unto remission of sins; saying, Repent ye: for the kingdom of heaven is at hand.

4 For this is he that was spoken of by Isaiah the prophet, saying,

The voice of one crying in the wilderness,

Make ye ready the way of the Lord,

Make his paths straight.

5 Every valley shall be filled,

And every mountain and hill shall be brought low;

And the crooked shall become straight,

And the rough ways smooth;

6 And all flesh shall see the salvation of God.

7 Now John himself had his raiment of camel's hair, and a leathern girdle about his loins; and his food was locusts and wild honey.

8 Then went out unto him Jerusalem, and all Judæa and all the region round about Jordan;

9 And they were baptized of him in the river Jordan, confessing their sins.

10 But when he saw many of the Pharisees and Sadducees coming to his baptism, he said unto them, Ye offspring of vipers, who warned you to flee from the wrath to come?

11 Bring forth therefore fruit worthy of repentance:

12 And think not to say within yourselves, We have Abraham to our father: for I say unto you, that God is able of these stones to raise up children unto Abraham.

13 And even now is the

axe laid unto the root of the trees: every tree therefore that bringeth not forth good fruit is hewn down, and cast into the fire.

14 I indeed baptize you with water unto repentance: but he that cometh after me is mightier than I, whose shoes I am not worthy to bear: he shall baptize you with the Holy Ghost and *with* fire.

15 Whose fan is in his hand, and he will thoroughly cleanse his threshing-floor; and he will gather his wheat into the garner, but the chaff he will burn up with unquenchable fire.

### JESUS BAPTIZED BY JOHN.
#### January A. D. 27.

16 Then cometh Jesus from Galilee to the Jordan unto John, to be baptized of him.

17 But John would have hindered him, saying, I have need to be baptized of thee, and comest thou to me?

18 But Jesus answering said unto him, Suffer *it* now:
for thus it becometh us to fulfil all righteousness. Then he suffereth him.

19 And Jesus, when he was baptized, went up straightway from the water: and praying, and lo, the heavens were opened unto him, and he saw the Spirit of God descending as a dove, and coming upon him;

20 And lo, a voice out of the heavens, saying, This is my beloved Son, in whom I am well pleased.

### THE TEMPTATION.

21 And Jesus, full of the Holy Spirit, returned from the Jordan, and was led by the Spirit in the wilderness during forty days, being tempted of the devil.

22 And he was with the wild beasts; and he did eat nothing in those days: and when they were completed, he hungered.

23 And the tempter came and said unto him, If thou art the Son of God, command that these stones become bread.

GET THEE HENCE, SATAN.

24 But he answered and said, It is written, Man shall not live by bread alone, but by every word that proceedeth out of the mouth of God.

25 Then the devil taketh him into the holy city; and he set him on the pinnacle of the temple, and saith unto him,

26 If thou art the Son of God, cast thyself down: for it is written,

He shall give his angels charge concerning thee:

And on their hands they shall bear thee up,

Lest haply thou dash thy foot against a stone.

27 Jesus said unto him, Again it is written, Thou shalt not tempt the Lord thy God.

28 Again, the devil taketh him unto an exceeding high mountain, and showeth him all the kingdoms of the world, and the glory of them;

29 And he said unto him, All these things will I give thee, if thou wilt fall down and worship me.

30 Then saith Jesus unto him, Get thee hence, Satan: for it is written, Thou shalt worship the Lord thy God, and him only shalt thou serve.

31 Then the devil leaveth him; and behold, angels came and ministered unto him.

32 And Jesus came into Galilee, preaching the gospel of God, and saying, The time is fulfilled, and the kingdom of God is at hand: repent ye, and believe in the gospel.

33 And he taught in their synagogues, being glorified of all.

34 And Jesus himself, when he began *to teach*, was about thirty years of age,

35 And John beareth witness of him, and crieth, saying, This was he of whom I said, He that cometh after me is become before me: for he was before me.

36 For of his fulness we all received, and grace for grace.

37 For the law was given by Moses; grace and truth came by Jesus Christ.

38 No man hath seen God at any time; the only begotten Son, which is in the bosom of the Father, he hath declared *him*.

39 And this is the witness of John, when the Jews sent unto him from Jerusalem priests and Levites to ask him, Who art thou?

40 And he confessed, and denied not; and he confessed, I am not the Christ.

41 And they asked him, What then? Art thou Elijah? And he saith, I am not. Art thou the prophet?

42 And he answered, No. They said therefore unto him, Who art thou? that we may give an answer to them that sent us. What sayest thou of thyself?

43 He said, I am the voice of one crying in the wilderness, Make straight the way of the Lord, as said Isaiah the prophet.

44 And they had been sent from the Pharisees.

45 And they asked him, and said unto him, Why then baptizest thou, if thou art not the

46 Christ, neither Elijah, neither the prophet?

47 John answered them, saying, I baptize with water: in the midst of you standeth one whom ye know not,

48 *Even* he that cometh after me, the latchet of whose shoe I am not worthy to unloose.

49 These things were done in Bethany beyond Jordan, where John was baptizing.

50 On the morrow he seeth Jesus coming unto him, and saith, Behold, the Lamb of God, which taketh away the sin of the world!

51 This is he of whom I said, After me cometh a man which is become before me: for he was before me.

52 And I knew him not; but that he should be made manifest to Israel, for this

cause came I baptizing with water.

53 And John bare witness, saying, I have beheld the Spirit descending as a dove out of heaven; and it abode upon him.

54 And I knew him not: but he that sent me to baptize with water, he said unto me, Upon whomsoever thou shalt see the Spirit descending, and abiding upon him, the same is he that baptizeth with the Holy Spirit.

55 And I have seen, and have borne witness that this is the Son of God.

## CHAPTER VII.

AGAIN on the morrow John was standing, and two of his disciples; and he looked upon Jesus as he walked, and saith, Behold, the Lamb of God!

2 And the two disciples heard him speak, and they followed Jesus.

3 And Jesus turned, and beheld them following, and saith unto them, What seek ye? And they said unto him, Rabbi (which is to say, being interpreted, Master), where abidest thou ?

4 He saith unto them, Come, and ye shall see. They came therefore and saw where he abode; and they abode with him that day: it was about the tenth hour.

5 One of the two that heard John *speak*, and followed him, was Andrew, Simon Peter's brother.

6 He findeth first his own brother, Simon, and saith unto him, We have found the Messiah (which is, being interpreted, Christ).

7 He brought him unto Jesus. Jesus looked upon him, and said, Thou art Simon the son of John: thou shalt be called Cephas (which is by interpretation, Peter).

8 On the morrow he was minded to go forth into Galilee, and he findeth Philip: and Jesus saith unto him, Follow me.

9 Now Philip was from Bethsaida, of the city of Andrew and Peter.

10 Philip findeth Nathanael, and saith unto him, We have found him, of whom Moses in the law, and the prophets, did write, Jesus of Nazareth, the son of Joseph.

11 And Nathanael said unto him, Can any good thing come out of Nazareth? Philip saith unto him, Come and see.

12 Jesus saw Nathanael coming to him, and saith of him, Behold, an Israelite indeed, in whom is no guile!

13 Nathanael saith unto him, Whence knowest thou me? Jesus answered and said unto him, Before Philip called thee, when thou wast under the fig tree, I saw thee.

14 Nathanael answered him, Rabbi, thou art the Son of God; thou art King of Israel.

15 Jesus answered and said unto him, Because I said unto thee, I saw thee underneath the fig tree, believest thou? thou shalt see greater things than these.

16 And he saith unto him, Verily, verily, I say unto you, Ye shall see the heaven opened, and the angels of God ascending and descending upon the Son of man.

### WATER MADE INTO WINE.
#### February, A. D. 27.

17 And the third day there was a marriage in Cana of Galilee; and the mother of Jesus was there: and Jesus also was bidden, and his disciples, to the marriage.

18 And when the wine failed, the mother of Jesus saith unto him, They have no wine.

19 And Jesus saith unto her, Woman, what have I to do with thee? mine hour is not yet come.

20 His mother saith unto the servants, Whatsoever he saith unto you, do it.

21 Now there were six waterpots of stone set there after the Jews' manner of purifying, containing two or three firkins apiece.

THE WEDDING AT CANA

22 Jesus saith unto them, Fill the waterpots with water. And they filled them up to the brim.

23 And he saith unto them, Draw out now, and bear unto the ruler of the feast. And they bare it.

24 And when the ruler of the feast tasted the water now become wine, and knew not whence it was (but the servants which had drawn the water knew), the ruler of the feast calleth the bridegroom,

25 And saith unto him, Every man setteth on first the good wine; and when *men* have drunk freely, *then* that which is worse: thou hast kept the good wine until now.

26 This beginning of his signs did Jesus in Cana of Galilee, and manifested his glory; and his disciples believed on him.

#### THE MONEY CHANGERS DRIVEN OUT.
April, A D 27.

27 After this he went down to Capernaum, he, and his mother, and *his* brethren, and his disciples: and there they abode not many days.

28 And the passover of the Jews was at hand, and Jesus went up to Jerusalem.

29 And he found in the temple those that sold oxen and sheep and doves, and the changers of money sitting.

30 And he made a scourge of cords, and cast all out of the temple, both the sheep and the oxen; and he poured out the changers' money, and overthrew their tables;

31 And to them that sold the doves he said, Take these things hence; make not my Father's house a house of merchandise.

32 His disciples remembered that it was written, The zeal of thine house shall eat me up.

33 The Jews therefore answered and said unto him, What sign shewest thou unto

us, seeing that thou doest these things?

34 Jesus answered and said unto them, Destroy this temple, and in three days I will raise it up.

35 The Jews therefore said, Forty and six years was this temple in building, and wilt thou raise it up in three days?

36 But he spake of the temple of his body.

37 When therefore he was raised from the dead, his disciples remembered that he spake this; and they believed the scripture, and the word which Jesus had said.

38 Now when he was in Jerusalem at the passover, during the feast, many believed on his name, beholding his signs which he did.

39 But Jesus did not trust himself unto them, for that he knew all men,

40 And because he needed not that any one should bear witness concerning man; for he himself knew what was in man.

## CHAPTER VIII.

### REGENERATION.

April, A. D. 27.

NOW there was a man of the Pharisees, named Nicodemus, a ruler of the Jews:

2 The same came to him by night, and said to him, Rabbi, we know that thou art a teacher come from God: for no man can do these signs that thou doest, except God be with him.

3 Jesus answered and said unto him, Verily, verily, I say unto thee, Except a man be born anew, he cannot see the kingdom of God.

4 Nicodemus saith unto him, How can a man be born when he is old? can he enter a second time into his mother's womb, and be born?

5 Jesus answered, Verily, verily, I say unto thee, Except a man be born of water and the Spirit, he cannot enter into the kingdom of God.

6 That which is born of

the flesh is flesh; and that which is born of the Spirit is spirit.

7 Marvel not that I said unto thee, Ye must be born anew.

8 The wind bloweth where it listeth, and thou hearest the voice thereof, but knowest not whence it cometh, and whither it goeth: so is every one that is born of the Spirit.

9 Nicodemus a n s w e r e d and said unto him, How can these things be?

10 Jesus answered and said unto him, Art thou the teacher of Israel, and understandest not these things?

11 Verily, verily, I say unto thee, We speak that we do know, and bear witness of that we have seen; and ye receive not our witness.

12 If I told you earthly things, and ye believe not, how shall ye believe, if I tell you heavenly things?

13 And no man hath ascended into heaven, but he that descended out of heaven, *even* the Son of man, which is in heaven.

14 And as Moses lifted up the serpent in the wilderness, even so must the Son of man be lifted up:

15 That whosoever believeth may in him have eternal life.

16 For God so loved the world, that he gave his only begotten Son, that whosoever believeth o n h i m should not perish, but have eternal life.

17 For God sent not the Son into the world to judge the world; but that the world should b e s a v e d through him.

18 He that believeth on him is not judged: he that believeth not hath been judged already, because he hath not believed on the name of the only begotten Son of God.

19 And this is the judgment, that the light is come into the world, and men loved the darkness rather

than the light; for their works were evil.

20 For every one that doeth ill hateth the light, and cometh not to the light, lest his works should be reproved.

21 But he that doeth the truth cometh to the light, that his works may be made manifest, that they have been wrought in God.

22 After these things came Jesus and his disciples into the land of Judæa; and there he tarried with them, and baptized.

23 And John also was baptizing in Ænon near to Salim, because there was much water there: and they came, and were baptized.

24 For John was not yet cast into prison.

25 There arose therefore a questioning on the part of John's disciples with a Jew about purifying.

26 And they came unto John, and said to him, Rabbi, he that was with thee beyond Jordan, to whom thou hast borne witness, behold, the same baptizeth, and all men come to him.

27 John answered, and said, A man can receive nothing, except it have been given him from heaven.

28 Ye yourselves bear me witness, that I said, I am not the Christ, but, that I am sent before him.

29 He that hath the bride is the bridegroom: but the friend of the bridegroom, which standeth and heareth him, rejoiceth greatly because of the bridegroom's voice: this my joy therefore is fulfilled.

30 He must increase, but I must decrease.

31 He that cometh from above is above all: he that is of the earth is of the earth, and of the earth he speaketh: he that cometh from heaven is above all.

32 What he hath seen and heard, of that he beareth witness; and no man receiveth his witness.

33 He that hath received

JOHN THE BAPTIST AT THE RIVER JORDAN.

his witness hath set his seal to *this*, that God is true.

34 For he whom God hath sent speaketh the words of God: for he giveth not the Spirit by measure.

35 The Father loveth the Son, and hath given all things into his hand.

36 He that believeth on the Son hath eternal life; but he that obeyeth not the Son shall not see life, but the wrath of God abideth on him.

## CHAPTER IX.

### THE WOMAN OF SAMARIA.

#### December, A.D. 27.

HEROD the tetrarch, being reproved by John for Herodias, his brother's wife, and for all the evil things which Herod had done, added yet this above all, that he shut up John in prison.

2 When therefore the Lord knew how that the Pharisees had heard that Jesus was making and baptizing more disciples than John (although Jesus himself baptized not, but his disciples) and had heard that John was cast into prison, he left Judæa, and departed again into Galilee.

3 And he must needs pass through Samaria.

4 And he cometh to a city of Samaria, called Sychar, near to the parcel of ground that Jacob gave to his son Joseph: and Jacob's well was there.

5 Jesus therefore, being wearied with his journey, sat thus by the well. It was about the sixth hour.

6 There cometh a woman of Samaria to draw water: Jesus saith unto her, Give me to drink. For his disciples were gone away into the city to buy food.

7 The Samaritan woman therefore saith unto him, How is it that thou, being a Jew, askest drink of me, which am a Samaritan woman? (For Jews have no dealings with Samaritans.)

8 Jesus answered and said unto her, If thou knewest the

gift of God, and who it is that saith to thee, Give me to drink; thou wouldest have asked of him, and he would have given thee living water.

9 The woman saith unto him, Sir, thou hast nothing to draw with, and the well is deep: from whence then hast thou that living water?

10 Art thou greater than our father Jacob, which gave us the well, and drank thereof himself, and his sons, and his cattle?

11 Jesus answered and said unto her, Every one that drinketh of this water shall thirst again:

12 But whosoever drinketh of the water that I shall give him shall never thirst; but the water that I shall give him shall become in him a well of water springing up unto eternal life.

13 The woman saith unto him, Sir, give me this water, that I thirst not, neither come all the way hither to draw.

14 Jesus saith unto her, Go, call thy husband, and come hither.

15 The woman answered and said unto him, I have no husband. Jesus saith unto her, Thou saidst well, I have no husband:

16 For thou hast had five husbands; and he whom thou now hast is not thy husband: this hast thou said truly.

17 The woman saith unto him, Sir, I perceive that thou art a prophet.

18 Our fathers worshipped in this mountain; and ye say, that in Jerusalem is the place where men ought to worship.

19 Jesus saith unto her, Woman, believe me, the hour cometh, when neither in this mountain, nor in Jerusalem, shall ye worship the Father.

20 Ye worship that which ye know not: we worship that which we know: for salvation is from the Jews.

21 But the hour cometh, and now is, when the true

JESUS AND THE SAMARITAN WOMAN AT THE WELL.

worshippers shall worship the Father in spirit and truth: for such doth the Father seek to be his worshippers.

22 God is a Spirit: and they that worship him must worship in spirit and truth.

23 The woman saith unto him, I know that Messiah cometh (which is called Christ): when he is come, he will declare unto us all things.

24 Jesus saith unto her, I that speak unto thee am *he*.

25 And upon this came his disciples; and they marvelled that he was speaking with a woman; yet no man said, What seekest thou? or, Why speakest thou with her?

26 So the woman left her waterpot, and went away into the city, and saith to the men, Come, see a man, which told me all things that *ever* I did: can this be the Christ?

27 They went out of the city, and were coming to him.

28 In the mean while the disciples prayed him, saying, Rabbi, eat.

29 But he said unto them, I have meat to eat that ye know not.

30 The disciples therefore said one to another, Hath any man brought him *aught* to eat?

31 Jesus saith unto them, My meat is to do the will of him that sent me, and to accomplish his work.

32 Say not ye, There are yet four months, and *then* cometh the harvest? behold, I say unto you, Lift up your eyes, and look on the fields, that they are white already unto harvest.

33 He that reapeth receiveth wages, and gathereth fruit unto life eternal; that he that soweth and he that reapeth may rejoice together.

34 For herein is the saying true, One soweth, and another reapeth.

35 I sent you to reap that whereon ye have not laboured: others have laboured, and ye are entered into their labour.

36 And from that city many of the Samaritans believed on him because of the word of the woman, who testified, He told me all things that *ever* I did.

37 So when the Samaritans came unto him, they besought him to abide with them: and he abode there two days.

38 And many more believed because of his word; and they said to the woman, Now we believe, not because of thy speaking: for we have heard for ourselves, and know that this is indeed the Saviour of the world.

39 And after the two days he went forth from thence into Galilee.

40 For Jesus himself testified, that a prophet hath no honour in his own country.

41 When he came into Galilee, the Galilæans received him, having seen all things that he did in Jerusalem at the feast: for they also went unto the feast.

### THE CHILD CURED.
December, A.D. 27.

42 He came therefore again unto Cana of Galilee, where he made the water wine. And there was a certain nobleman, whose son was sick at Capernaum.

43 When he heard that Jesus was come out of Judæa into Galilee, he went unto him, and besought *him* that he would come down, and heal his son; for he was at the point of death.

44 Jesus therefore said unto him, Except ye see signs and wonders, ye will in no wise believe.

45 The nobleman saith unto him, Sir, come down ere my child die.

46 Jesus saith unto him, Go thy way; thy son liveth. The man believed the word that Jesus spake unto him, and he went his way.

47 And as he was now going down, his servants met him, saying, that his son lived.

48 So he inquired of them

"Come Sit By Me When Told Me All Things That Ever I Did."

the hour when he began to amend. They said therefore unto him, Yesterday at the seventh hour the fever left him.

49 So the father knew that *it was* at that hour in which Jesus said unto him, Thy son liveth: and himself believed, and his whole house.

50 This is again the second sign that Jesus did, having come out of Judæa into Galilee.

## CHAPTER X.

### JESUS READS ISAIAH.

#### April, A.D. 28.

AND Jesus returned in the power of the Spirit into Galilee: and a fame went out concerning him through all the region round about.

2 And he taught in their synagogues, being glorified of all.

3 And he came to Nazareth, where he had been brought up: and he entered, as his custom was, into the synagogue on the sabbath day, and stood up to read.

4 And there was delivered unto him the book of the prophet Isaiah. And he opened the book, and found the place where it was written,

5 The Spirit of the Lord is upon me,

Because he anointed me to preach good tidings to the poor:

He hath sent me to proclaim release to the captives,

And recovering of sight to the blind,

To set at liberty them that are bruised,

To proclaim the acceptable year of the Lord.

6 And he closed the book, and gave it back to the attendant, and sat down: and the eyes of all in the synagogue were fastened on him.

7 And he began to say unto them, To-day hath this scripture been fulfilled in your ears.

8 And all bare him witness, and wondered at the words of grace which proceeded out of his mouth:

9 And were astonished, and said, Whence hath this man this wisdom, and these mighty works?

10 Is not this the carpenter's son? is not his mother called Mary? and his brethren, James, and Joseph, and Simon, and Judas?

11 And his sisters, are they not all with us? Whence then hath this man all these things?

12 And they were offended in him. But Jesus said unto them, A prophet is not without honour, save in his own country, and in his own house.

13 And he could there do no mighty work, save that he laid his hands upon a few sick folk, and healed them. And he marvelled because of their unbelief.

14 And he said unto them, Doubtless ye will say unto me this parable, Physician, h e a l thyself: whatsoever we have heard done at Capernaum, do also here in thine own country.

15 And he said, Verily I say unto you, No prophet is acceptable in his own country.

16 But of a truth I say unto you, There were many widows in Israel in the days of Elijah, when the heaven was shut up three years and six months, when there came a great famine over all the land;

17 And unto none of them was Elijah sent, but only to Zarephath, in the land of Sidon, unto a woman that was a widow.

18 And there were many lepers in Israel in the time of Elisha the prophet; and none of them was cleansed, but only Naaman the Syrian.

19 And they were all filled with wrath in the synagogue, as they heard these things;

20 And they rose up, and cast him forth out of the city, and led him unto the brow of the hill whereon their city was built, that they might throw him down headlong.

21 But he passing through

JESUS PREACHING HIS FIRST SERMON AT NAZARETH.

the midst of them went his way.

22 And leaving Nazareth, he went round about the villages teaching, and he came and dwelt in Capernaum, which is by the sea, in the borders of Zebulun and Naphtali:

A.D. 28.

23 That it might be fulfilled which was spoken by Isaiah the prophet, saying,

24 The land of Zebulun and the land of Naphtali,

Toward the sea, beyond Jordan,

Galilee of the Gentiles,

25 The people which sat in darkness

Saw a great light,

And to them which sat in the region and shadow of death,

To them did light spring up.

26 And they were astonished at his teaching; for his word was with authority.

27 And Jesus walking by the sea of Galilee, saw two brethren, Simon who is called Peter, and Andrew his brother, casting a net into the sea; for they were fishers.

28 And he saith unto them, Come ye after me, and I will make you fishers of men.

29 And they straightway left the nets, and followed him.

30 And going on from thence he saw other two brethren, James the *son* of Zebedee, and John his brother, in the boat with Zebedee their father, mending their nets; and he called them.

31 And they straightway left the boat and their father, and followed him.

EVIL SPIRITS CAST OUT.

32 And they go into Capernaum; and straightway on the sabbath day he entered into the synagogue and taught.

33 And they were astonished at his teaching: for he taught them as having authority, and not as the scribes.

34 And there was in their synagogue a man with an unclean spirit;

35 And he cried out, saying, What have we to do with thee, thou Jesus of Nazareth? art thou come to destroy us? I know thee who thou art, the Holy One of God.

36 And Jesus rebuked him, saying, Hold thy peace, and come out of him.

37 And the unclean spirit, tearing him and crying with a loud voice, came out of him.

38 And they were all amazed, insomuch that they questioned among themselves, saying, What is this? a new teaching! with authority he commandeth even the unclean spirits, and they obey him.

39 And the report of him went out straightway everywhere into all the region of Galilee round about.

40 And straightway, when they were come out of the synagogue, they came into the house of Simon and Andrew, with James and John.

A.D. 28.

41 Now Simon's wife's mother lay sick of a fever; and straightway they tell him of her:

42 And he came and took her by the hand, and raised her up; and the fever left her, and she ministered unto them.

43 And when the sun was setting, all they that had any sick with divers diseases brought them unto him; and he laid his hands on every one of them, and healed them.

44 And devils also came out from many, crying out, and saying, Thou art the Son of God. And rebuking them, he suffered them not to speak, because they knew that he was the Christ.

45 And in the morning, a great while before day, he arose up and went out, and departed into a desert place, and there prayed.

46 And Simon and they

THE HEALING OF PETER'S WIFE'S MOTHER.

that were with him followed after him;

47 And they found him, and say unto him, All are seeking thee.

48 And he saith unto them, Let us go elsewhere into the next towns, that I may preach there also; for to this end came I forth.

49 But the multitudes sought after him, and came unto him, and would have stayed him, that he should not go from them.

50 He said unto them, I must preach the good tidings of the kingdom of God to the other cities also: for therefore was I sent.

April and May, A.D. 28

51 And Jesus went about in all Galilee, teaching in their synagogues, and preaching the gospel of the kingdom, and healing all manner of disease and all manner of sickness among the people.

52 And the report of him went forth into all Syria: and they brought unto him all that were sick, holden with divers diseases and torments, possessed with devils, and epileptic, and palsied: and he healed them.

53 And there followed him great multitudes from Galilee and Decapolis and Jerusalem and Judæa and *from* beyond Jordan.

## CHAPTER XI.

### THE LEPER CLEANSED.

#### A.D. 28.

AND it came to pass, while he was in one of the cities, behold, a man full of leprosy : and when he saw Jesus, he fell on his face, and besought him, saying, Lord, if thou wilt, thou canst make me clean.

2 And Jesus, moved with compassion, stretched forth his hand, and touched him, and saith unto him, I will; be thou made clean.

3 And straightway the leprosy departed from him, and he was made clean.

4 And he strictly charged him, and straightway sent him out,

5 And saith unto him, See thou say nothing to any man: but go thy way, shew thyself to the priest, and offer for thy cleansing the things which Moses commanded, for a testimony unto them.

6. But he went out, and began to publish it much, and to spread abroad the matter, insomuch that Jesus could no more openly enter into a city, but was without in desert places:

7 And so much the more went abroad the report concerning him: and great multitudes came together to hear, and to be healed of their infirmities.

8 And he withdrew himself in the deserts, and prayed.

### THE PALSIED CURED.

9 And when he entered again into Capernaum after some days, it was noised that he was in the house.

10 And many were gathered together, so that there was no longer room *for them*, no, not even about the door: and he spake the word unto them.

11 And there were Pharisees and Doctors of the law sitting by, which were come out of every village of Galilee and Judæa and Jerusalem: and the power of the Lord was with him to heal.

12 And behold, men bring on a bed a man that was palsied: and they sought to bring him in, and to lay him before him.

13 And not finding by what *way* they might bring him in because of the multitude, they went up to the housetop, and let him down through the tiles with his couch into the midst before Jesus.

A.D. 28.

14 And Jesus seeing their faith saith unto the sick of the palsy, Son, be of good cheer; thy sins are forgiven.

But there were certain of the scribes sitting there, and reasoning in their hearts,

"Depart From Me, for I am a Sinful Man."

Why doth this man thus speak? he blasphemeth: who can forgive sins but one, *even* God?

16 And straightway Jesus, perceiving in his spirit that they so reasoned within themselves, saith unto them, Why reason ye these things in your hearts?

17 Whether is easier, to say to the sick of the palsy, Thy sins are forgiven; or to say, Arise, and take up thy bed, and walk?

18 But that ye may know that the Son of man hath power on earth to forgive sins (he saith to the sick of the palsy), I say unto thee, Arise, take up thy bed, and go unto thy house.

19 And immediately he rose up before them, and took up that whereon he lay, and departed to his house, glorifying God.

20 And amazement took hold on all, and they glorified God; and they were filled with fear, saying, We have seen strange things to-day.

21 And Jesus with his disciples withdrew to the sea; and a great multitude from Galilee followed:

THE DRAUGHT OF FISHES.

22 Now it came to pass, while the multitude pressed upon him and heard the word of God, that he was standing by the lake of Gennesaret;

23 And he saw two boats standing by the lake: but the fishermen had gone out of them, and were washing their nets.

24 And he entered into one of the boats, which was Simon's, and asked him to put out a little from the land.

And he sat down and taught the multitudes out of the boat.

April, A.D. 28.

25 And when he had left speaking, he said unto Simon, Put out into the deep, and let down your nets for a draught.

26 And Simon answered and said, Master, we toiled all night, and took nothing:

but at thy word I will let down the nets.

27 And when they had this done, they inclosed a great multitude of fishes; and their nets were breaking;

28 And they beckoned unto their partners in the other boat, that they should come and help them. And they came, and filled both the boats, so that they began to sink.

29 But Simon Peter, when he saw it, fell down at Jesus' knees, saying, Depart from me; for I am a sinful man, O Lord.

30 For he was amazed, and all that were with him, at the draught of the fishes which they had taken;

31 And so were also James and John, sons of Zebedee, which were partners with Simon.

32 And Jesus said unto Simon, Fear not; from henceforth thou shalt catch men.

33 And when they had brought their boats to land, they left all, and followed him.

34 And after these things he went forth, and beheld a publican, Levi, named Matthew the *son* of Alphæus sitting at the place of toll, and he saith unto him, Follow me.

35 And he forsook all, and rose up and followed him.

36 And Levi made him a great feast in his house:

37 And it came to pass, as Jesus sat at meat in the house, behold, many publicans and sinners came and sat down with him and his disciples.

38 And the Pharisees and their scribes murmured against his disciples, saying, Why do ye eat and drink with the publicans and sinners?

39 Why eateth your Master with the publicans and sinners?

40 And Jesus answering said unto them, They that are whole have no need of a

"Henceforth Thou Shalt Catch Men."

physician; but they that are sick.

41 But go ye and learn what *this* meaneth, I desire mercy, and not sacrifice: for I came not to call the righteous, but sinners to repentance.

42 Then come to him the disciples of John, saying, Why do we and the Pharisees fast oft, but thy disciples fast not?

43 And Jesus said unto them, Can the sons of the bride-chamber m o u r n, as long as the bridegroom is with them? but the days will come, when the bridegroom shall be taken away from them, and then will they fast.

44 And he spake also a parable unto them; No man seweth a piece of undressed cloth on an old garment: else that which should fill it up taketh from it, the new from the old, and a worse rent is made.

45 Neither do *men* put new wine into old wine-skins:

else the skins burst, and the wine is spilled, and the skins perish: but they put new wine into fresh wine-skins, and both are preserved.

46 And no man having drunk old *wine* desireth new: for he saith, The old is good.

## CHAPTER XII.
### THE POOL OF BETHESDA.
#### Spring, A.D. 28.

AFTER these t h i n g s there was a feast of the Jews; and Jesus went up to Jerusalem.

2 Now there is in Jerusalem by the sheep *gate* a pool, which is called in Hebrew B e t h e s d a, having five porches.

3 In these lay a multitude of them that were sick, blind, halt, withered.

4 And a certain man was there, which had been thirty and eight years in his infirmity.

5 When Jesus saw him lying, and knew that he had been now a long time *in that*

*case*, he saith unto him, Wouldest t h o u be made whole?

6 The sick man answered him, Sir, I have no man, when the water is troubled, to put me into the pool: but while I am coming, another steppeth down before me.

7 Jesus saith unto him, Arise, take up thy bed, and walk.

8 And straightway the man was made whole, and took up his bed and walked.

9 Now it was the sabbath on that day.

10 So the Jews said unto him that was cured, It is the sabbath, and it is not lawful for thee to take up thy bed.

11 But he answered them, He that made me whole, the same said unto me, Take up thy bed, and walk.

12 They asked him, Who is the man that said unto thee, Take up *thy bed*, and walk?

13 But he that was healed wist not who it was; for Jesus had conveyed himself away, a multitude being in the place.

14 Afterward Jesus findeth him in the temple, and said unto him, Behold, thou art made whole; sin no more, lest a worse thing befall thee.

15 The man went away, and told the Jews that it was Jesus which had made him whole.

16 And for this cause did the Jews persecute Jesus, because he did these things on the sabbath.

17 But Jesus answered them, My Father worketh even until now, and I work.

18 For this cause therefore the Jews sought the more to kill him, because he not only brake the sabbath, but also called God his own Father, making himself equal with God.

19 Jesus therefore answered and said unto them,

Verily, verily, I say unto you, The Son can do nothing of himself, but what he seeth the Father doing: for what

"Wilt Thou be Made Whole?"

things soever he doeth, these the Son also doeth in like manner.

20 For the Father loveth the Son, and sheweth him all things that himself doeth: and greater works than these will he shew him, that ye may marvel.

21 For as the Father raiseth the dead and quickeneth them, even so the Son also quickeneth whom he will.

22 For neither doth the Father judge any man, but he hath given all judgement unto the Son;

23 That all may honour the Son, even as they honour the Father. He that honoureth not the Son honoureth not the Father which sent him.

24 Verily, verily, I say unto you, He that heareth my word, and believeth him that sent me, hath eternal life, and cometh not into judgement, but hath passed out of death into life.

25 Verily, verily, I say unto you, The hour cometh, and now is when the dead shall hear the voice of the Son of God; and they that hear shall live.

26 For as the Father hath life in himself, even so gave he to the Son also to have life in himself:

27 And he gave him authority to execute judgement because he is the Son of man.

28 Marvel not at this: for the hour cometh, in which all that are in the tombs shall hear his voice,

29 And shall come forth; they that have done good, unto the resurrection of life; and they that have done ill unto the resurrection of judgement.

30 I can of myself do nothing: as I hear, I judge: and my judgement is righteous; because, I seek not mine own will, but the will of him that sent me.

· 31 If I bear witness of myself my witness is not true.

32 It is another that bear-

eth witness of me; and I know that the witness which he witnesseth of me is true.

33 Ye have sent unto John, and he hath borne witness unto the truth.

34 But the witness which I receive is not from man: howbeit I say these things, that ye may be saved.

35 He was the lamp that burneth and shineth: and ye were willing to rejoice for a season in his light.

36 But the witness which I have is greater than *that of* John: for the works which the Father hath given me to accomplish, the very works that I do, bear witness of me, that the Father hath sent me.

37 And the Father which sent me, he hath borne witness of me. Ye have neither heard his voice at any time, nor seen his form.

38 And ye have not his word abiding in you: for whom he sent, him ye believe not.

39 Ye search the scrip-tures, because ye think that in them ye have eternal life: and these are they which bear witness of me;

40 And ye will not come to me, that ye may have life.

41 I receive not glory from men.

42 But I know you, that ye have not the love of God in yourselves.

43 I am come in my Fathers name, and ye receive me not: if another shall come in his own name, him ye will receive.

44 How can ye believe, which receive glory one of another, and the glory that *cometh* from the only God ye seek not?

45 Think not that I will accuse you to the Father: there is one that accuseth you, *even* Moses, on whom ye have set your hope.

46 For if ye believed Moses, ye would believe me; for he wrote of me.

47 But if ye believe not his writings, how shall ye believe my words?

"If Ye Believed Moses, Ye Would Believe Me."

## CHAPTER XIII.

### THE SABBATH MADE FOR MAN.

#### May, A.D. 28.

NOW it came to pass on a sabbath, that he was going through the cornfields; and his disciples plucked the ears of corn, and did eat, rubbing them in their hands.

2 But the Pharisees, when they saw it, said unto him, Behold, thy disciples do that which is not lawful to do upon the sabbath.

3 And Jesus answering them said, Have ye not read even this, what David did, when he was an hungred, he, and they that were with him;

4 How he entered into the house of God when Abiathar was high priest, and did eat the shewbread, which it is not lawful to eat save for the priests, and gave also to them that were with him?

5 Or have ye not read in the law, how that on the sabbath day the priests in the temple profane the sabbath, and are guiltless?

6 But I say unto you, that one greater than the temple is here.

7 But if ye had known what this meaneth, I desire mercy, and not sacrifice, ye would not have condemned the guiltless.

8 And he said unto them, The sabbath was made for man, and not man for the sabbath:

9 So that the Son of man is lord even of the sabbath.

### THE WITHERED HAND.

#### June, A.D. 28.

10 And it came to pass on another sabbath, that he entered into the synagogue and taught: and there was a man there, and his right hand was withered.

11 And the scribes and the Pharisees watched him, whether he would heal on the sabbath; that they might find how to accuse him.

12 And they asked him, saying, Is it lawful to heal on the sabbath day?

13 But he knew their

thoughts; and he said to the man that had his hand withered, Rise up, and stand forth in the midst.

14 And he arose and stood forth.

15 And Jesus said unto them, I ask you, Is it lawful on the sabbath to do good, or to do harm? to save a life, or to destroy it?

16 But they held their peace.

17 And he said unto them, What man shall there be of you, that shall have one sheep, and if this fall into a pit on the sabbath day, will he not lay hold on it, and lift it out?

18 How much then is a man of more value than a sheep! Wherefore it is lawful to do good on the sabbath day.

19 And when he had looked round about on them with anger, being grieved at the hardening of their heart, he saith unto the man, Stretch forth thy hand.

20 And he stretched it forth; and it was restored whole, as the other.

21 But the Pharisees were filled with madness; and communed one with another what they might do to Jesus.

22 And went out, and straightway with the Herodians took counsel against him, how they might destroy him.

23 And Jesus perceiving *it* withdrew from thence: and many followed him; and he healed them all,

24 And a great multitude from Galilee followed: and from Judæa, and from Jerusalem, and from Idumæa, and beyond Jordan, and about Tyre and Sidon, hearing what great things he did, came unto him.

25 And he spake to his disciples, that a little boat should wait on him because of the crowd, lest they should throng him:

26 For he had healed many; insomuch that as many as had plagues pressed

JESUS RESTORES A WITHERED HAND.

upon him that they might touch him.

27 And the unclean spirits, whensoever t h e y beheld him, fell down before him, and cried, saying, Thou art the Son of God.

28 And he charged them much that they should not make him known.

29 That it might be fulfilled which was spoken by Isaiah the prophet, saying,

30 Behold, my servant whom I have chosen;

31 My beloved in whom my soul is well pleased:

32 I will put my Spirit upon him,

And he shall declare judgement to the Gentiles.

33 He shall not strive, nor cry aloud;

Neither shall any one hear his voice in the streets.

34 A bruised reed shall he not break,

And smoking flax shall he not quench,

Till he send forth judgement unto victory.

35 And in his name shall the Gentiles hope.

## CHAPTER XIV.
### ALL NIGHT IN PRAYER.
#### Midsummer, A. D. 28.

AND it came to pass in these days, that he went out into the mountain to pray; and he continued all night in prayer to God.

2 And when it was day, he called his disciples: and he chose from them twelve, whom also he named apostles;

3 That they might be with him, and that he might send them forth to preach, and to have authority to cast out devils:

4 Now the names of the twelve apostles are these:

5 The first, Simon, who is called Peter, and Andrew his brother; James the *son* of Zebedee, and J o h n his brother;

6 And them he surnamed Boanerges, which is, Sons of thunder:

7 P h i l i p and Bartholo-

mew, and Matthew the publican, and Thomas, and James *the son* of Alphæus, and Simon the Cananæan, which was called the Zealot, and Judas *the son* of James,

8 And Judas Iscariot, which also betrayed him.

9 And he came down with them, and stood on a level place, and a great multitude of his disciples, and a great number of the people from all Judæa and Jerusalem, and the sea coast of Tyre and Sidon, which came to hear him, and to be healed of their diseases;

10 And they that were troubled with unclean spirits were healed.

11 And all the multitude sought to touch him: for power came forth from him, and healed *them* all.

### THE SERMON ON THE MOUNT.
#### Midsummer, A.D. 28.

12 And seeing the multitudes, he went up into the mountains: and when he had sat down, his disciples came unto him: and he opened his mouth and taught them, saying,

13 Blessed are the poor in spirit: for theirs is the kingdom of heaven.

14 Blessed are they that mourn: for they shall be comforted.

15 Blessed are the meek: for they shall inherit the earth.

16 Blessed are they that hunger and thirst after righteousness: for they shall be filled.

17 Blessed are the merciful: for they shall obtain mercy.

18 Blessed are the pure in heart: for they shall see God.

19 Blessed are the peacemakers: for they shall be called sons of God.

20 Blessed are they that have been persecuted for righteousness' sake: for theirs is the kingdom of heaven.

21 Blessed are ye when *men* shall reproach you, and persecute you, and say all

THE HORNS OF HATTIN, THE MOUNT OF THE BEATITUDES.

manner of evil against you falsely, for my sake.

22 Rejoice, in that day, and leap *for joy:*

23 Rejoice, and be exceeding glad: for great is your reward in heaven: for so persecuted they the prophets which were before you.

24 But woe unto you that are rich! for ye have received your consolation.

25 Woe unto you, ye that are full now! for ye shall hunger.

26 Woe *unto you,* ye that laugh now! for you shall mourn and weep.

27 Woe *unto you,* when all men shall speak well of you! for in the same manner did their fathers to the false prophets.

28 Ye are the salt of the earth: but if the salt have lost its savour, wherewith shall it be salted? it is thenceforth good for nothing, but to be cast out and trodden under foot of men.

29 Ye are the light of the world. A city set on a hill cannot be hid.

30 Neither do *men* light a lamp, and put it under the bushel, but on the stand; and it shineth unto all that are in the house.

31 Even so let your light shine before men, that they may see your good works, and glorify your Father which is in heaven.

32 Think not that I came to destroy the law or the prophets: I came not to destroy, but to fulfill.

33 Verily I say unto you, Till heaven and earth pass away, one jot or one tittle shall in no wise pass away from the law, till all things be accomplished.

34 Whosoever therefore shall break one of these least commandments, and shall teach men so, shall be called least in the kingdom of heaven: but whosoever shall do and teach them, he shall be called great in the kingdom of heaven.

35 For I say unto you, that

except your righteousness shall exceed *the righteousness* of the scribes and Pharisees, ye shall in no wise enter into the kingdom of heaven.

36 Ye have heard that it was said to them of old time, Thou shalt not kill; and whosoever shall kill shall be in danger of the judgement:

37 But I say unto you, that every one who is angry with his brother shall be in danger of the judgement; and whosoever shall say to his brother, Raca, shall be in danger of the council; and whosoever shall say, Thou fool, shall be in danger of the hell of fire.

38 If therefore thou art offering thy gift at the altar, and there rememberest that thy brother hath aught against thee,

39 Leave there thy gift before the altar, and go thy way, first be reconciled to thy brother, and then come and offer thy gift.

40 Agree with thine adversary quickly, whiles thou art with him in the way; lest haply the adversary deliver thee to the judge, and the judge deliver thee to the officer, and thou be cast into prison.

41 Verily I say unto thee, Thou shalt by no means come out thence, till thou have paid the last farthing.

42 Ye have heard that it was said, Thou shalt not commit adultery:

43 But I say unto you, that every one that looketh on a woman to lust after her hath committed adultery with her already in his heart.

44 And if thy right eye causeth thee to stumble, pluck it out, and cast it from thee: for it is profitable for thee that one of thy members should perish, and not thy whole body be cast into hell.

45 And if thy right hand causeth thee to stumble, cut it off, and cast it from thee: for it is profitable for thee that one of thy members

THE SERMON ON THE MOUNT.

should perish, and not thy whole body go into hell.

46 It was said also, Whosoever shall put away his wife, let him give her a writing of divorcement:

47 But I say unto you, that every one that putteth away his wife, saving for the cause of fornication, maketh her an adultress: and whosoever shall marry her when she is put away committeth adultery.

48 Again, ye have heard that it was said to them of old time, Thou shalt not forswear thyself, but shalt perform unto the Lord thine oaths:

49 But I say unto you, Swear not at all; neither by the heaven, for it is the throne of God;

50 Nor by the earth, for it is the footstool of his feet; nor by Jerusalem, for it is the city of the great King.

51 Neither shalt thou swear by thy head, for thou canst not make one hair white or black.

52 But let your speech be, Yea, yea; Nay, nay: and whatsoever is more than these is of the evil *one*.

53 Ye have heard that it was said, An eye for an eye, and a tooth for a tooth:

54 But I say unto you, Resist not him that is evil: but whosoever smiteth thee on thy right cheek, turn to him the other also.

55 And if any man would go to law with thee, and take away thy coat, let him have thy cloke also.

56 And whosoever shall compel thee to go one mile, go with him twain.

57 Give to him that asketh thee, and from him that would borrow of thee turn not thou away.

58 And of him that taketh away thy goods ask them not again.

59 And as ye would that men should do to you, do ye also to them likewise.

60 Ye have heard that it was said, Thou shalt love thy neighbour, and hate thine enemy:

61 But I say unto you which hear, Love your enemies, do good to them that hate you, bless them that curse you, pray for them that despitefully use you and persecute you.

62 That ye may be sons of your Father which is in heaven: for he maketh his sun to rise on the evil and the good and sendeth rain on the just and the unjust.

63 For if ye love them that love you, what reward have ye? do not even the publicans the same?

64 And if ye salute your brethren only, what do ye more *than others?* do not even the Gentiles the same?

65 And if ye lend to them of whom ye hope to receive, what thank have ye? even sinners lend to sinners, to receive again as much.

66 But love your enemies, and do *them* good, and lend, never despairing; and your reward shall be great, and ye shall be sons of the Most High: for he is kind toward the unthankful and evil.

67 Be ye merciful, even as your Father is merciful.

68 Ye therefore shall be perfect, as your heavenly Father is perfect.

## CHAPTER XV.

TAKE heed that ye do not your righteousness before men, to be seen of them: else ye have no reward with your Father which is in heaven.

2 When therefore thou doest alms, sound not a trumpet before thee, as the hypocrites do in the synagogues and in the streets, that they may have glory of men. Verily I say unto you, They have received their reward.

3 But when thou doest alms, let not thy left hand know what thy right hand doeth:

4 That thine alms may be in secret: and thy Father which seeth in secret shall recompense thee.

5 And when ye pray, ye

PRAYER IN SECRET.

shall not be as the hypocrites: for they love to stand and pray in the synagogues and in the corners of the streets, that they may be seen of men. Verily I say unto you, They have received their reward.

6 But thou, when thou prayest, enter into thine inner chamber, and having shut thy door, pray to thy Father which is in secret, and thy Father which seeth in secret shall recompense thee.

7 And in praying use not vain repetitions, as the Gentiles do: for they think that they shall be heard for their much speaking.

8 Be not therefore like unto them: for your Father knoweth what things ye have need of, before ye ask him.

9 After this manner therefore pray ye: Our Father which art in heaven, Hallowed be thy name.

10 Thy kingdom come. Thy will be done, as in heaven, so on earth.

11 Give us this day our daily bread.

12 And forgive us our debts, as we also have forgiven our debtors.

13 And bring us not into temptation, but deliver us from the evil *one*.

14. For thine is the kingdom, and the power, and the glory, for ever. Amen.
[Supplied from A. V.]

15 For if ye forgive men their trespasses, your heavenly Father will also forgive you.

16 But if ye forgive not men their trespasses, neither will your Father forgive your trespasses.

17 Moreover when ye fast, be not, as the hypocrites, of a sad countenance: for they disfigure their faces, that they may be seen of men to fast. Verily I say unto you, They have received their reward.

18 But thou, when thou fastest, anoint thy head, and wash thy face;

19 That thou be not seen of men to fast, but of thy

Father which is in secret: and thy Father which seeth in secret, shall recompense thee.

20 Lay not up for yourselves treasures upon the earth, where moth and rust doth consume, and where thieves break through and steal:

21 But lay up for yourselves treasures in heaven, where neither moth nor rust doth consume, and where thieves do not break through nor steal:

20 For where thy treasure is, there will thy heart be also.

23 The lamp of the body is the eye: if therefore thine eye be single, thy whole body shall be full of light.

24 But if thine eye be evil, thy whole body shall be full of darkness. If therefore the light that is in thee be darkness, how great is the darkness!

25 No man can serve two masters: for either he will hate the one, and love the other; or else he will hold to one, and despise the other. Ye cannot serve God and mammon.

26 Therefore I say unto you, Be not anxious for your life, what ye shall eat, or what ye shall drink; nor yet for your body, what ye shall put on. Is not the life more than the food, and the body than the raiment?

27 Behold the birds of the heaven, that they sow not, neither do they reap, nor gather into barns; and your heavenly Father feedeth them. Are not ye of much more value than they?

28 And which of you by being anxious can add one cubit unto his stature?

29 And why are ye anxious concerning raiment? Consider the lilies of the field, how they grow; they toil not, neither do they spin:

30 Yet I say unto you, that even Solomon in all his glory was not arrayed like one of these.

31 But if God doth so

THE SEA OF GALILEE FROM THE NORTH.

clothe the grass of the field, which to-day is, and to-morrow is cast into the oven, *shall he* not much more *clothe* you, O ye of little faith?

32 Be not therefore anxious, saying, What shall we eat? or, What shall we drink? or, Wherewithal shall we be clothed?

33 For after all these things do the Gentiles seek; for your heavenly Father knoweth that ye have need of all these things.

34 But seek ye first his kingdom, and his righteousness; and all these things shall be added unto you.

35 Be not therefore anxious for the morrow: for the morrow will be anxious for itself. Sufficient unto the day is the evil thereof.

## CHAPTER XVI.

JUDGE not, that ye be not judged. For with what judgement ye judge, ye shall be judged: and with what measure ye mete, it shall be measured unto you.

2 And why beholdest thou the mote that is in thy brothers eye, but considerest not the beam that is in thine own eye?

3 Or how wilt thou say to thy brother, Let me cast out the mote out of thine eye; and lo, the beam is in thine own eye?

4 Thou hypocrite, cast out first the beam out of thine own eye; and then shalt thou see clearly to cast out the mote out of thy brother's eye.

5 Give not that which is holy unto the dogs, neither cast your pearls before the swine, lest haply they trample them under their feet, and turn and rend you.

6 Ask, and it shall be given you; seek, and ye shall find; knock, and it shall be opened unto you:

7 For every one that asketh receiveth; and he that seeketh findeth; and to him that knocketh it shall be opened.

8 Or what man is there of

you, who, if his son shall ask him for a loaf, will give him a stone;

9 Or if he shall ask for a fish, will give him a serpent?

10 If ye then, being evil, know how to give good gifts unto your children, how much more shall your Father which is in heaven give good things to them that ask him?

11 All things therefore whatsoever ye would that men should do unto you, even so do ye also unto them: for this is the law and the prophets.

12 Enter ye in by the narrow gate: for wide is the gate, and broad is the way, that leadeth to destruction, and many be they that enter in thereby.

13 For narrow is the gate, and straitened the way, that leadeth unto life, and few be they that find it.

14 Beware of false prophets, which come to you in sheep's clothing, but inwardly are ravening wolves.

15 By their fruits ye shall know them. Do *men* gather grapes of thorns, or figs of thistles?

16 Even so every good tree bringeth forth good fruit; but the corrupt tree bringeth forth evil fruit.

17 A good tree cannot bring forth evil fruit, neither can a corrupt tree bring forth good fruit.

18 The good man out of the good treasure of his heart bringeth forth that which is good; and the evil *man* out of the evil *treasure* bringeth forth that which is evil: for out of the abundance of the heart his mouth speaketh.

19 Therefore by their fruits ye shall know them.

20 Every tree that bringeth not forth good fruit is hewn down, and cast into the fire.

21 And why call ye me, Lord, Lord, and do not the things which I say?

22 Not every one that saith unto me, Lord, Lord, shall enter into the kingdom of

THE HOUSE OF THE FOOLISH MAN DESTROYED.

heaven; but he that doeth the will of my Father which is in heaven.

23 Many will say to me in that day, Lord, Lord, did we not prophesy by thy name, and by thy name cast out devils, and by thy name do many mighty works?

24 And then will I profess unto them, I never knew you: depart from me, ye that work iniquity.

25 Every one therefore which heareth these words of mine, and doeth them, shall be likened unto a wise man, which built his house upon the rock:

26 And the rain descended, and the floods came, and the winds blew, and beat upon that house; and it fell not: for it was founded upon the rock.

27 And every one that heareth these words of mine, and doeth them not, shall be likened unto a foolish man, which built his house upon the sand:

28 And the rain descended, and the floods came, and the winds blew, and smote upon that house; and it fell: and great was the fall thereof.

29 And it came to pass, when Jesus ended these words, the multitudes were astonished at his teaching.

30 For he taught them as *one* having authority, and not as their scribes.

## CHAPTER XVII.
### THE CENTURION'S FAITH.
#### Midsummer, A.D. 28.

AFTER he had ended all his sayings in the ears of the people, he entered into Capernaum.

2 And a certain centurion's servant, who was dear unto him, was sick and at the point of death.

3 And when he heard concerning Jesus, he sent unto him elders of the Jews, asking him that he would come and save his servant.

4 And saying, Lord, my servant lieth in the house sick of the palsy, grievously tormented.

5 And they, when they came to Jesus, besought him earnestly, saying, He is worthy that thou shouldest do this for him:

6 For he loveth our nation, and himself built us our synagogue.

7 And Jesus saith, I will come and heal him.

8 And when he was now not far from the house, the centurion sent friends to him, saying unto him, Lord, trouble not thyself: for I am not worthy that thou shouldest come under my roof:

9 Wherefore neither thought I myself worthy to come unto thee: but say the word, and my servant shall be healed.

10 For I also am a man set under authority, having under myself soldiers: and I say to this one, Go, and he goeth; and to another, Come, and he cometh; and to my servant, Do this, and he doeth it.

11 And when Jesus heard these things, he marvelled at him, and turned and said unto the multitude that followed him, I say unto you, I have not found so great faith, no, not in Israel.

12 And I say unto you, that many shall come from the east and the west, and shall sit down with Abraham, and Isaac, and Jacob, in the kingdom of heaven:

13 But the sons of the kingdom shall be cast forth into the outer darkness: there shall be the weeping and gnashing of teeth.

14 And Jesus said, Go thy way; as thou hast believed, *so* be it done unto thee, and the servant was healed in that hour.

THE WIDOW'S SON.

15 And it came to pass soon afterwards, that he went to a city called Nain; and his disciples went with him, and a great multitude.

16 Now when he drew near to the gate of the city, behold there was carried out one that was dead, the only son of his mother, and she was a widow: and much people of the city was with her.

THE WIDOW'S SON RESTORED TO LIFE.

17 And when the Lord saw her, he had compassion on her, and said unto her, Weep not.

18 And he came nigh and touched the bier: and the bearers stood still. And he said, Young man, I say unto thee, Arise.

19 And he that was dead sat up, and began to speak. And he gave him to his mother.

20 And fear took hold on all: and they glorified God, saying, A great prophet is arisen among us: and, God hath visited his people.

21 And this report went forth concerning him in the whole of Judæa, and all the region round about.

22 And the disciples of John told him of all these things.

23 And John calling unto him two of his disciples sent them to the Lord, saying, Art thou he that cometh, or look we for another?

Midsummer, A. D. 28.

24 And when the men were come unto him, they said, John the Baptist hath sent us unto thee, saying, Art thou he that cometh, or look we for another?

25 In that hour he cured many of diseases and plagues and evil spirits; and on many that were blind bestowed sight.

26 And he answered and said unto them, Go your way, and tell John what things ye have seen and heard; the blind receive their sight, the lame walk, the lepers are cleansed, and the deaf hear, the dead are raised up, the poor have good tidings preached to them.

27 And blessed is he, whosoever shall find none occasion of stumbling in me.

28 And when the messengers of John were departed, he began to say unto the multitudes concerning John, What went ye out into the wilderness to behold? a reed shaken with the wind?

29 But what went ye out to see? a man clothed in soft

raiment? Behold, they which are gorgeously apparelled, and live delicately are in kings' courts.

30 But what went ye out to see? a prophet? Yea, I say unto you, and much more than a prophet.

31 This is he of whom it is written,

Behold, I sent my messenger before thy face,

Who shall prepare thy way before thee.

32 Verily I say unto you, Among them that are born of women there hath not arisen a greater than John the Baptist: yet he that is but little in the kingdom of heaven is greater than he.

33 And from the days of John the Baptist until now the kingdom of heaven suffereth violence, and men of violence take it by force.

34 For all the prophets and the law prophesied until John.

35 And if ye are willing to receive *it*, this is Elijah, which is to come.

36 He that hath ears to hear, let him hear.

37 And all the people when they heard, and the publicans, justified God, being baptised with the baptism of John.

38 But the Pharisees and the lawyers rejected for themselves the counsel of God, being not baptised of him.

39 And the Lord said: Whereunto then shall I liken the men of this generation, and to what are they like?

40 They are like unto children that sit in the marketplace, and call one to another; which say, We piped unto you, and ye did not dance; we wailed, and ye did not weep.

41 For John the Baptist is come eating no bread nor drinking wine; and ye say, He hath a devil.

42 The Son of man is come eating and drinking; and ye say, Behold, a gluttonous man, and a winebibber, a

"Come Unto Me."

friend of publicans and sinners!

43 But wisdom is justified of all her children.

44 Then began he to upbraid the cities wherein most of his mighty works were done, because they repented not.

45 Woe unto thee, Chorazin! woe unto thee, Bethsaida! for if the mighty works had been done in Tyre and Sidon which were done in you, they would have repented long ago in sackcloth and ashes.

46 Howbeit I say unto you, it shall be more tolerable for Tyre and Sidon in the day of judgement, than for you.

47 And thou, Capernaum, shalt thou be exalted unto heaven? thou shalt go down unto Hades: for if the mighty works had been done in Sodom which were done in thee, it would have remained until this day.

48 Howbeit I say unto you, that it shall be more tolerable for the land of Sodom in the day of judgement, than for thee.

49 At that season Jesus answered and said, I thank thee, O Father, Lord of heaven and earth, that thou didst hide these things from the wise and understanding, and didst reveal them unto babes:

50 Yea, Father, for so it was well-pleasing in thy sight.

51 All things have been delivered unto me of my Father: and no one knoweth the Son, save the Father; neither doth any know the Father, save the Son, and he to whomsoever the Son willeth to reveal *him*.

52 Come unto me, all ye that labour and are heavy laden, and I will give you rest.

53 Take my yoke upon you, and learn of me; for I am meek and lowly in heart: and ye shall find rest unto your souls.

54 For my yoke is easy, and my burden is light.

## CHAPTER XVIII.

### THE WOMAN A SINNER.

AND one of the Pharisees desired him that he would eat with him. And he entered into the Pharisee's house, and sat down to meat.

2 And behold, a woman which was in the city, a sinner; and when she knew that Jesus was sitting at meat in the Pharisee's house, she brought an alabaster cruse of ointment.

3 And standing behind at his feet, weeping, she began to wet his feet with her tears, and wiped them with the hair of her head, and kissed his feet, and anointed them with the ointment.

4 Now when the Pharisee which had bidden him saw it, he spoke within himself, saying, This man, if he were a prophet, would have perceived who and what manner of woman this is which toucheth him, that she is a sinner.

5 And Jesus answering said unto him, Simon, I have somewhat to say unto thee. And he saith, Master, say on.

6 A certain lender had two debtors: the one owed five hundred pence, and the other fifty.

7 When they had not *wherewith* to pay, he forgave them both. Which of them therefore will love him most?

8 Simon answered a n d said, He, I suppose, to whom he forgave the most. And he said unto him, Thou hast rightly judged.

9 And turning to the woman, he said unto Simon, Seest thou this woman? I entered into thine house, thou gavest me no water for my feet: but she hath wetted my feet with her tears, and wiped them with her hair.

10 Thou gavest me no kiss: but she, since the time I came in, hath not ceased to kiss my feet.

11 My head with oil thou didst not anoint: but she

" THY SINS ARE FORGIVEN."

hath anointed my feet with ointment.

12 Wherefore I say unto thee, Her sins, which are many, are forgiven; for she loved much: but to whom little is forgiven, *the same* loveth little.

13 And he said unto her, Thy sins are forgiven.

14 And they that sat at meat with him began to say within themselves, Who is this that even forgiveth sins?

15 And he said unto the woman, Thy faith hath saved thee; go in peace.

BLASPHEMY.

16 And it came to pass soon afterwards, that he went about through cities and villages, preaching and bringing the good tidings of the kingdom of God, and with him the twelve,

17 And certain women which had been healed of evil spirits and infirmities, Mary that was called Magdalene, from whom seven devils had gone out,

18 And Joanna the wife of Chuza Herod's steward, and Susanna and many others, which ministered unto them of their substance.

19 And he cometh into a house.

20 And the multitude cometh together again, so that they could not so much as eat bread.

21 And when his friends heard it, they went out to lay hold on him: for they said, He is beside himself.

Autumn, A. D. 28.

22 Then was brought unto him one possessed with a devil, blind and dumb: and he healed him, insomuch that the dumb man spake and saw.

23 And all the multitudes were amazed, and said, Is this the son of David?

24 But when the Pharisees heard it, they said, This man doth not cast out devils, but by Beelzebub the prince of the devils.

25 But he, knowing their thoughts, said unto them, Every kingdom divided

against itself is brought to desolation; and a house *divided* against a house falleth,

26 And if Satan also is divided against himself, how shall his kingdom stand? because ye say that I cast out devils by Beelzebub.

27 And if 1 by Beelzebub cast out devils, by whom do your sons cast them out? therefore shall they be your judges.

28 But if I by the finger of God cast out devils, then is the kingdom of God come upon you.

29 When the strong *man* fully armed guardeth his own court, his goods are in peace:

30 But when a stronger than he shall come upon him, and overcome him, he taketh from him his whole armour wherein he trusted, and divideth his spoils.

31 He that is not with me is against me; and he that gathereth not with me scattereth.

32 Verily I say unto you,

All their sins shall be forgiven unto the sons of men, and their blasphemies wherewith soever they shall blaspheme:

33 But whosoever shall blaspheme against the Holy Spirit hath never forgiveness but is guilty of an eternal sin:

34 And whosoever shall speak a word against the Son of man, it shall be forgiven him;

35 But whosoever shall speak against the Holy Spirit, it shall not be forgiven him, neither in this world, nor in that which is to come.

36 Because they said, He hath an unclean spirit.

37 Either make the tree good, and its fruit good; or make the tree corrupt, and its fruit corrupt: for the tree is known by its fruit.

38 Ye offspring of vipers, how can ye, being evil, speak good things? for out of the abundance of the heart the mouth speaketh.

39 The good man out of

his good treasure bringeth forth good things: and the evil man out of his evil treasure bringeth forth evil things.

40 And I say unto you, that every idle word that men shall speak, they shall give account thereof in the day of judgment.

41 For by thy words thou shalt be justified, and by thy words thou shalt be condemned.

## THE PHARISEES DENOUNCED.

42 Then certain of the scribes and Pharisees answered him, saying, Master, we would see a sign from thee.

43 But he answered and said unto them, An evil and adulterous generation seeketh after a sign; and there shall no sign be given to it but the sign of Jonah the prophet.

44 For as Jonah was three days and three nights in the belly of the whale; so shall the Son of man be three days and three nights in the heart of the earth.

45 The men of Nineveh shall stand up in the judgement with this generation, and shall condemn it: for they repented at the preaching of Jonah; and behold, a greater than Jonah is here.

46 The queen of the south shall rise up in the judgement with this generation, and shall condemn it: for she came from the ends of the earth to hear the wisdom of Solomon; and behold, a greater than Solomon is here.

47 No man, when he hath lighted a lamp, covereth it with a vessel, or putteth it under a bed; but putteth it on a stand, that they which enter in may see the light.

48 The lamp of the body is the eye: if therefore thine eye be single, thy whole body shall be full of light.

49 But if thine eye be evil, thy whole body shall be full of darkness. If therefore the light that is

in thee be darkness, how great is the darkness!

50 Look therefore whether the light that is in thee be not darkness.

51 If therefore thy whole body be full of light, having no part dark, it shall be wholly full of light, as when the lamp with its bright shining doth give thee light.

52 The unclean spirit, when he is gone out of the man, passeth through waterless places, seeking rest, and findeth it not.

53 Then he saith, I will return into my house whence I came out; and when he is come, he findeth it empty, swept, and garnished.

54 Then goeth he, and taketh with himself seven other spirits more evil than himself, and they enter in and dwell there: and the last state of that man becometh worse than the first.

55 Even so shall it be also unto this evil generation.

Autumn, A. D. 28.

56 While he was yet speaking to the multitudes, behold, his mother and his brethren stood without, seeking to speak to him.

57 And they could not come at him for the crowd.

58 And one said unto him, Behold, thy mother and thy brethren stand without, seeking to speak to thee.

59 But he answered and said unto him that told him, Who is my mother? and who are my brethren?

60 And he stretched forth his hand towards his disciples, and said, Behold, my mother and my brethren!

61 My mother and my brethren are these which hear the word of God, and do it.

62 For whosoever shall do the will of my Father which is in heaven, he is my brother, and sister, and mother.

## CHAPTER XIX.

NOW as he spake, a Pharisee asketh him to dine with him: and he went in and sat down to meat.

"BEHOLD MY MOTHER AND MY BRETHREN."

2 And when the Pharisee saw it, he marvelled that he had not first washed before dinner.

3 And the Lord said unto him, Now do ye Pharisees cleanse the outside of the cup and of the platter; but your inward part is full of extortion and wickedness.

4 Ye foolish ones, did not he that made the outside make the inside also?

5 Howbeit give for alms those things which are within; and behold, all things are clean unto you.

6 But woe unto you Pharisees! for ye tithe mint and rue and every herb, and pass over judgement and the love of God: but these ought ye to have done, and not to leave the other undone.

7 Woe unto you Pharisees! for ye love the chief seats in the synagogues, and the salutations in the market-places.

8 Woe unto you! for ye are as the tombs which appear not, and the men that walk over *them* know it not.

9 And one of the lawyers answering saith unto him, Master, in saying this thou reproachest us also.

10 And he said, Woe unto you lawyers also! for ye lade men with burdens grievous to be borne, and ye yourselves touch not the burdens with one of your fingers.

11 Woe unto you! for ye build the tombs of the prophets, and your fathers killed them.

12 So ye are witnesses and consent unto the works of your fathers: for they killed them, and ye build *their tombs.*

13 Therefore also said the wisdom of God, I will send unto them prophets and apostles; and *some* of them they shall kill and persecute;

14 That the blood of all the prophets, which was shed from the foundation of the' world, may be required of this generation;

15 From the blood of Abel unto the blood of Zachariah, who perished between the altar and the sanctuary: yea, I say unto you, it shall be required of this generation.

16 Woe unto you lawyers! for ye took away the key of knowledge: ye entered not in yourselves, and them that were entering in ye hindered.

17 And when he was come out from thence, the scribes and the Pharisees began to press upon *him* vehemently, and to provoke him to speak of many things;

18 Laying wait for him, to catch something out of his mouth.

19 In the mean time, when the many thousands of the multitude were gathered together, insomuch that they trode one upon another, he began to say unto his disciples first of all, Beware ye of the leaven of the Pharisees, which is hypocrisy.

20 There is nothing covered up, that shall not be revealed: and hid, that shall not be known.

21 Wherefore whatsoever ye have said in the darkness shall be heard in the light; and what ye have spoken in the ear in the inner chambers shall be proclaimed upon the housetops.

22 And I say unto you my friends, Be not afraid of them which kill the body, and after that have no more that they can do.

23 But I will warn you whom ye shall fear: Fear him, which after he hath killed hath power to cast into hell; yea, I say unto you, Fear him.

24 Are not five sparrows sold for two farthings? and not one of them is forgotten in the sight of God.

25 But the very hairs of your head are all numbered. Fear not: ye are of more value than many sparrows.

26 And I say unto you, Every one who shall confess me before men, him shall the Son of man also con-

THE RICH FOOL.

fess before the angels of God:

27 But he that denieth me in the presence of men shall be denied in the presence of the angels of God.

28 And when they bring you before the synagogues, and the rulers, and the authorities, be not anxious how or what ye shall answer, or what ye shall say:

29 For the Holy Spirit shall teach you in that very hour what ye ought to say.

30 And one out of the multitude said unto him, Master, bid my brother divide the inheritance with me.

31 But he said unto him, Man, who made me a judge or a divider over you?

32 And he said unto them, Take heed, and keep yourselves from all covetousness: for a man's life consisteth not in the abundance of the things which he possesseth.

33 And he spake a parable unto them, saying, The ground of a certain rich man brought forth plentifully:

34 And he reasoned within himself, saying, What shall I do, because I have not where to bestow my fruits?

35 And he said, This will I do: I will pull down my barns, and build greater; and there will I bestow all my corn and my goods.

36 And I will say to my soul, Soul, thou hast much goods laid up for many years; take thine ease, eat, drink, be merry.

37 But God said unto him, Thou foolish one, this night is thy soul required of thee; and the things which thou hast prepared, whose shall they be?

38 So is he that layeth up treasure for himself, and is not rich toward God.

39 And he said unto his disciples, Therefore I say unto you, Be not anxious for *your* life, what ye shall eat; nor yet for your body, what ye shall put on.

40 For the life is more than the food, and the body than the raiment.

41 Consider the ravens, that they sow not, neither reap; which have no store-chamber nor barn; and God feedeth them: of how much more value are ye than the birds!

42 And which of you by being anxious can add a cubit unto his stature?

43 If then ye are not able to do even that which is least, why are ye anxious concerning the rest?

44 Consider the lilies, how they grow: they toil not, neither do they spin; yet I say unto you, Even Solomon in all his glory was not arrayed like one of these.

45 But if God doth so clothe the grass in the field, which to-day is, and to-morrow is cast into the oven; how much more *shall he clothe* you, O ye of little faith?

46 And seek not ye what ye shall eat, and what ye shall drink, neither be ye of doubtful mind.

47 For all these things do the nations of the world seek after: but your Father knoweth that ye have need of these things.

48 Howbeit seek ye his kingdom, and these things shall be added unto you.

49 Fear not, little flock; for it is your Father's good pleasure to give you the kingdom.

50 Sell that ye have, and give alms; make for yourselves purses which wax not old, a treasure in the heavens that faileth not, where no thief draweth near, neither moth destroyeth.

51 For where your treasure is, there will your heart be also.

52 Let your loins be girded about, and your lamps burning;

53 And be ye yourselves like unto men looking for their lord, when he shall return from the marriage feast; that, when he cometh and knocketh, they may straightway open unto him.

54 Blessed are those ser-

GOD SAID UNTO HIM, "THOU FOOLISH ONE."

vants, whom the Lord when he cometh shall find watching: verily I say unto you, that he shall gird himself, and make them sit down to meat, and shall come and serve them.

55 And if he shall come in the second watch, and if in the third, and find *them* so, blessed are those *servants*.

56 But know this, that if the master of the house had known in what hour the thief was coming, he would have watched, and not have left his house to be broken through.

57 Be ye also ready: for in an hour that ye think not the Son of man cometh.

58 And Peter said, Lord, speakest thou this parable unto us, or even unto all?

59 And the Lord said, Who then is the faithful and wise steward, whom his lord shall set over his household, to give them their portion of food in due season?

60 Blessed is that servant, whom his lord when he cometh shall find so doing.

61 Of a truth I say unto you, that he will set him over all that he hath.

62 But if that servant shall say in his heart, My lord delayeth his coming; and shall begin to beat the menservants and the maidservants, and to eat and drink, and to be drunken;

63 The lord of that servant shall come in a day when he expecteth not, and in an hour when he knoweth not, and shall cut him asunder, and appoint his portion with the unfaithful.

64 And that servant, which knew his lord's will, and made not ready, nor did according to his will, shall be beaten with many *stripes*;

65 But he that knew not, and did things worthy of stripes, shall be beaten with few *stripes*.

66 And to whomsoever much is given, of him shall much be required: and to whom they commit much

of him will they ask the more.

67 I came to cast fire upon the earth; and what will I if it is already kindled?

68 But I have a baptism to be baptized with; and how am I straitened till it be accomplished!

69 Think ye that I am come to give peace in the earth? I tell you, Nay; but rather division:

70 For there shall be from henceforth five in one house divided, three against two, and two against three.

71 They shall be divided father against son, and son against father; mother against daughter, and daughter against her mother; mother in law against her daughter in law, and daughter in law against her mother in law.

72 And he said to the multitudes also, When ye see a cloud rising in the west, straightway ye say, There cometh a shower; and so it cometh to pass.

73 And when *ye see* a south wind blowing, ye say, There will be a scorching heat; and it cometh to pass.

74 Ye hypocrites, ye know how to interpret the face of the earth and the heaven, but how is it that ye know not how to interpret this time?

75 And why even of yourselves judge ye not what is right?

76 For as thou art going with thine adversary before the magistrate, on the way give diligence to be quit of him; lest haply he hale thee unto the judge, and the judge shall deliver thee to the officer, and the officer shall cast thee into prison.

77 I say unto thee, Thou shalt by no means come out thence, till thou have paid the very last mite.

78 Now there were some present at that very season which told him of the Galilæans, whose blood Pilate had mingled with their sacrifices.

79 And he answered and

JESUS PREACHING BY THE SEA OF GALILEE.

said unto them, Think ye that these Galilæans were sinners above all the Galilæans, because they have suffered these things?

80 I tell you, Nay: but, except ye repent, ye shall all in like manner perish.

81 Or those eighteen, upon whom the tower in Siloam fell, and killed them, think ye that they were offenders above all the men that dwell in Jerusalem?

82 I tell you, Nay: but, except ye repent, ye shall all likewise perish.

83 And he spake this parable; A certain man had a fig tree planted in his vineyard; and he came seeking fruit there on, and found none.

84 And he said unto the vinedresser, Behold, t h e s e three years I come seeking fruit on this fig tree, and find none: cut it down; why doth it also cumber the ground?

85 And he answering saith unto him, Lord, let it alone this year also, till I shall dig about it, and dung it:

86 And if it bear fruit thenceforth, *well*; but if not, thou shalt cut it down.

## CHAPTER XX.

### THE PARABLES.

#### Autumn, A. D. 28.

ON that day went Jesus out of the house, and sat by the sea-side.

2 And there were gathered unto him great multitudes, so that he entered into a boat, and sat; and all the multitude stood on the beach.

3 And he spake to them many things in parables, saying, Behold, the sower went forth to sow;

4 And as he sowed, some *seeds* fell by the wayside, and the birds came and devoured them:

5 And others fell upon the rocky places, where they had not much earth: and straightway they sprang up, because they had no deepness of earth:

6 And when the sun was risen, they were scorched,

and because they had no root, they withered away.

7 And others fell upon the thorns; and the thorns grew up, and choked them:

8 And others fell upon the good ground, and yielded fruit, some a hundredfold, some sixty, some thirty.

9 He that hath ears, let him hear.

10 Another parable set he before them, saying, The kingdom of heaven is likened unto a man that sowed good seed in his field:

11 But while men slept, his enemy came and sowed tares also among the wheat, and went away.

12 But when the blade sprang up, and b r o u g h t forth fruit, then appeared the tares also.

13 And the servants of the householder came and said unto him, Sir, didst thou not sow good seed in thy field? whence then hath it tares?

14 And he said unto them, An enemy hath done this. And the servants say unto him, Wilt thou then that we go and gather them up?

15 But he saith, Nay; lest haply while ye gather up the tares, ye root up the wheat with them.

16 Let both grow together until the harvest: and in the time of the harvest I will say to the reapers, Gather up first the tares, and bind them in bundles to burn them: but gather the wheat into my barn.

17 And he said, So is the kingdom of God, as if a man should cast seed upon the earth;

18 And should sleep and rise night and day, and the seed should spring up and grow, he knoweth not how.

19 The earth beareth fruit of herself; first the blade, then the ear, then the full corn in the ear.

20 But when the fruit is ripe, straightway he putteth forth the sickle, because the harvest is come.

21 Another parable set he before them, saying, The

"Behold, the Sower Went Forth to Sow."

kingdom of heaven is like unto a grain of mustard seed, which a man took, and sowed in his field:

22 Which indeed is less than all seeds; but when it is grown, it is greater than the herbs, and becometh a tree, so that the birds of the heaven come and lodge in the branches thereof.

23 Another parable spake he unto them: The kingdom of heaven is like unto leaven, which a woman took, and hid in three measures of meal, till it was all leavened.

24 All these things spake Jesus in parables unto the multitudes; and without a parable spake he nothing unto them:

25 That it might be fulfilled which was spoken by the prophet, saying,

I will open my mouth in parables;

I will utter things hidden from the foundation of the world.

26 And the disciples came, and said unto him, Why speakest thou unto them in parables?

27 And he answered and said unto them, Unto you it is given to know the mysteries of the kingdom of heaven, but to them it is not given.

28 For whosoever hath, to him shall be given, and he shall have abundance: but whosoever hath not, from him shall be taken away even that which he hath.

29 Therefore speak I to them in parables; because seeing they see not, and hearing they hear not, neither do they understand.

30 And unto them is fulfilled the prophecy of Isaiah, which saith,

By hearing ye shall hear, and shall in no wise understand;

And seeing ye shall see, and shall in no wise perceive:

31 For this people's heart is waxed gross,

And their ears are dull of hearing,

And their eyes they have closed;

Lest haply they should perceive with their eyes,

And hear with their ears,

32 And understand with their heart,

And should turn again,

And I should heal them.

33 But blessed are your eyes, for they see; and your ears, for they hear.

34 For verily I say unto you, that many prophets and righteous men desired to see the things which ye see, and saw them not; and to hear the things which ye hear, and heard them not.

35 And when he was alone, they that were about him with the twelve asked of him the parables.

36 And he said, the parable of the sower is this:

37 The seed is the word of God.

38 The sower soweth the word.

39 And those by the way side are they that have heard; then cometh the devil, and taketh away the word from their heart, that they may not believe and be saved.

40 And those on the rock *are* they which, when they have heard, receive the word with joy; and these have no root, which for a while believe, and in time of temptation fall away.

41 And that which fell among the thorns, these are they that have heard, and as they go on their way they are choked with cares and riches and pleasures of *this* life, and bring no fruit to perfection.

42 And that in the good ground, these are such as in an honest and good heart, having heard the word, hold it fast, and bring forth fruit with patience, some a hundredfold, some sixty, some thirty.

43 And he said unto them, Is the lamp brought to be put under the bushel, or under the bed, *and* not to be put on the stand?

44 For there is nothing hid, save that it should be manifested, neither was *anything* made secret, but that it should come to light.

45 Take heed therefore how ye hear: for whosoever hath, to him shall be given; and whosoever hath not, from him shall be taken away even that which he thinketh he hath.

46 And the disciples say unto him, Explain unto us the parable of the tares of the field.

47 And he answered and said, He that soweth the good seed is the Son of man; and the field is the world;

48 The good seed, these are the sons of the kingdom; and the tares are the sons of the evil *one;*

49 And the enemy that sowed them is the devil: and the harvest is the end of the world; and the reapers are angels.

50 As therefore the tares are gathered up and burned with fire; so shall it be in the end of the world.

51 The Son of man shall send forth his angels, and they shall gather out of his kingdom all things that cause stumbling, and them that do iniquity, and shall cast them into the furnace of fire: there shall be the weeping and gnashing of teeth.

52 Then shall the righteous shine forth as the sun in the kingdom of their Father. He that hath ears, let him hear.

53 The kingdom of heaven is like unto a treasure hidden in the field; which a man found, and hid; and in his joy he goeth and selleth all that he hath, and buyeth that field.

54 Again, the kingdom of heaven is like unto a man that is a merchant seeking goodly pearls:

55 And having found one pearl of great price, he went and sold all that he had, and bought it.

56 Again, the kingdom of heaven is like unto a net, that was cast into the sea, and gathered of every kind:

57 Which, when it was filled, they drew up on the beach; and they sat down, and gathered the good into vessels, but the bad they cast away.

58 So shall it be in the end of the world: the angels shall come forth, and sever the wicked from among the righteous,

59 And shall cast them into the furnace of fire: there shall be the weeping and gnashing of teeth.

60 Then said Jesus unto them, Have ye understood all these things? They say unto him, Yea.

61 And he said unto them, Therefore every scribe who hath been made a disciple to the kingdom of heaven is like unto a man that is a householder, which bringeth forth out of his treasure things new and old.

## CHAPTER XXI.

AND as they went in the way, a certain man said unto him, I will follow thee whithersoever thou goest.

2 And Jesus said unto him, The foxes have holes, and the birds of the heaven *have* nests; but the Son of man hath not where to lay his head.

3 And he said unto another, Follow me. But he said, Lord, suffer me first to go and bury my father.

4 But he said unto him, Leave the dead to bury their own dead ; but go thou and publish abroad the kingdom of God.

5 And another also said, I will follow thee, Lord; but first suffer me to bid farewell to them that are at my house.

6 But Jesus said unto him, No man, having put his hand to the plough, and looking back, is fit for the kingdom of God.

THE TEMPEST STILLED.

7 And on that day, when

THE PEARL OF GREAT PRICE.

even was come, he saith unto them, Let us go over unto the other side.

8 And leaving the multitude, they take him with them, even as he was, in the boat. And other boats were with him.

9 And there ariseth a great storm of wind, and the waves beat into the boat, insomuch that the boat was now filling.

10 And he himself was in the stern, asleep on the cushion; and they awake him, and say unto him, Master, carest thou not that we perish?

11 And he awoke, and rebuked the wind, and said unto the sea, Peace, be still. And the wind ceased, and there was a great calm.

12 And he said unto them, Why are ye fearful? have ye not yet faith?

13 And they feared exceedingly, and said one to another, Who then is this, that even the wind and the sea obey him?

### THE DEMONS ENTER INTO SWINE.
#### Autumn, A. D. 28.

14 And they came to the other side of the sea, into the country of the Gerasenes.

15 And when he was come out of the boat, straightway there met him out of the tombs a man with an unclean spirit, who had his dwelling in the tombs:

16 And no man could any more bind him, no, not with a chain;

17 Because that he had been often bound with fetters and chains, and the chains had been rent asunder by him, and the fetters broken in pieces: and no man had strength to tame him.

18 And always, night and day, in the tombs and in the mountains, he was crying out, and cutting himself with stones.

19 And when he saw Jesus from afar, he ran and worshipped him;

20 And crying out with a

loud voice, he saith, What have I to do with thee, Jesus, thou Son of the Most High God? I adjure thee by God, torment me not.

21 For he said unto him, Come forth, thou unclean spirit, out of the man.

22 For oftentimes it had seized him: and he was kept under guard, and bound with c h a i n s and fetters; and breaking the bands asunder, he was driven of the devil into the deserts.

23 And Jesus asked him, What is thy name? And he said, Legion; for many devils were entered into him.

24 And they intreated him that he would not command them to depart into the abyss.

25 Now there was there on the mountain side a great herd of swine feeding.

26 And they b e s o u g h t him, saying, Send us into the swine, that we may enter into them.

27 And he said unto them, Go. And the unclean spirits came out, and entered into the swine: and the herd rushed down the steep into the sea, *in number* about two thousand; and they were choked in the sea.

28 And when they that fed them saw what had come to pass, they fled, and told it in the city and in the country.

29 And behold, all the city came out to meet Jesus:

30 And they came and found the man, from whom the devils were gone out, sitting, clothed and in his right mind, at the feet of Jesus: and they were afraid.

31 And they that saw it declared unto them how it befell him that was possessed with devils, and concerning the swine.

32 And all the people of the country of the Garasenes round about asked him to depart from them; for they were holden with great fear:

33 And as he was entering into the boat, he that had been possessed with devils

THE DEMONIAC OF GADARA.

besought him that he might be with him.

34 And he suffered him not, but saith unto him, Go to thy house unto thy friends, and tell them how great things the Lord hath done for thee, and *how* he had mercy on thee.

35 And he went his way, and began to publish in Decapolis how great things Jesus had done for him: and all men did marvel.

36 And when Jesus h a d crossed over again in the boat unto the other side, the multitude welcomed him; for they were all waiting for him.

## CHAPTER XXII.

### JAIRUS' DAUGHTER.

Autumn, A. D. 28.

AND there cometh one of the rulers of the synagogue, Jairus by name; and seeing Jesus, he falleth at his feet,

2 And beseecheth him much, saying, My little daughter is at the point of

death: *I pray thee*, that thou come and lay thy hands on her, that she may be made whole, and live.

3 And Jesus arose, and followed him, and so *did* his disciples.

4 But as he went the multitudes thronged him.

### THE ISSUE OF BLOOD.

5 And behold, a woman, who had an issue of blood twelve years,

6 And had suffered many things of many physicians, and had spent all that she had, and was nothing bettered, but rather grew worse,

7 Having heard the things concerning Jesus, came in the crowd b e h i n d, a n d touched the border of his garment.

8 For she said, If I touch but his garments, I shall be made whole.

9 And straightway the fountain of her blood was dried up; and she felt in her body that she was healed of her plague.

10 And straightway Jesus,

perceiving in himself that the power *proceeding* from him had gone forth, turned him about in the crowd, and said, Who touched my garments?

11 And his disciples said unto him, Thou seest the multitude thronging thee, and sayest thou, Who touched me?

12 But Jesus said, Some one did touch me:

13 And when the woman saw that she was not hid, she came trembling, and falling down before him declared in the presence of all the people for what cause she touched him, and how she was healed immediately.

14 And he said unto her, Daughter, be of good cheer, thy faith hath made thee whole; go in peace, and be whole of thy plague.

15 And the woman was made whole from that hour.

16 While he yet spake, there cometh one from the ruler of the synagogue's *house,* saying, Thy daughter is dead; trouble not the Master.

17 But Jesus, not heeding the word spoken, saith unto the ruler of the synagogue, Fear not, only believe, and she shall be made whole.

18 And when he came to the house, he suffered not any man to enter in with him, save Peter, and John, and James, and the father of the maiden and her mother.

19 And when Jesus came into the ruler's house, and saw the flute-players, and the crowd making a tumult,

20 He saith unto them, Why make ye a tumult, and weep? Give place: for the damsel is not dead, but sleepeth.

21 And they laughed him to scorn, knowing that she was dead.

22 And taking the child by the hand, he saith unto her, Talitha cumi; which is, being interpreted, Damsel, I say unto thee, Arise.

23 And her spirit returned. And straightway the damsel

"Damsel, I say unto thee arise."

rose up, and walked; for she was twelve years old. And he commanded that *something* be given her to eat.

24 And her parents were amazed: And he charged them to tell no man what had been done.

25 But the fame hereof went forth into all that land.

### THE BLIND SEE AND THE DUMB SPEAK.

26 And as Jesus passed by from thence, two blind men followed him, crying out, and saying, Have mercy on us, thou son of David.

27 And when he was come into the house, the blind men came to him: and Jesus saith unto them, Believe ye that I am able to do this? They say unto him, Yea, Lord.

28 Then touched he their eyes, saying, According to your faith be it done unto you.

29 And their eyes were opened. And Jesus strictly charged them, saying, See that no man know it.

30 But they went forth, and spread abroad his fame in all that land.

31 And as they went forth, behold there was brought to him a dumb man possessed with a devil.

32 And when the devil was cast out, the dumb man spake; and the multitudes marvelled, saying, It was never so seen in Israel.

33 But the Pharisees said, By the prince of the devils casteth he out devils.

## CHAPTER XXIII.

### Winter, A. D. 29.

AND Jesus went about all the cities and the villages, teaching in their synagogues, and preaching the gospel of the kingdom, and healing all manner of disease and all manner of sickness.

2 But when he saw the multitudes, he was moved with compassion for them, because they were distressed and scattered, as sheep not having a shepherd.

3 Then saith he unto his disciples, The harvest truly is plenteous, but the labourers are few.

4 Pray ye therefore the Lord of the harvest, that he send forth labourers into his harvest.

THE TWELVE SENT OUT.

5 And he called unto him his twelve disciples, and gave them authority over unclean spirits, to cast them out, and to heal all manner of disease and all manner of sickness.

6 And he sent them forth by two and two, to preach the kingdom of God, and to heal the sick.

7 And charged them, saying, Go not into *any* way of the Gentiles, and enter not into any city of the Samaritans:

8 But go rather to the lost sheep of the house of Israel.

9 And as ye go, preach, saying, The kingdom of heaven is at hand.

10 Heal the sick, raise the dead, cleanse the lepers, cast out devils: freely ye received, freely give.

11 Get you no gold, nor silver, nor brass in your purses;

12 No wallet for *your* journey, neither two coats, nor shoes, nor staff: for the labourer is worthy of his food.

13 And into whatsoever city or village ye shall enter, search out who in it is worthy; and there abide till ye go forth.

14 And as ye enter into the house salute it.

15 And if the house be worthy, let your peace come upon it: but if it be not worthy, let your peace return to you.

16 And whatsoever place shall not receive you, and they hear you not, as ye go forth thence, shake off the dust that is under your feet for a testimony unto them.

17 Verily I say unto you, It shall be more tolerable for the land of Sodom and Go-

morrah in the day of judgement, than for that city.

18 Behold, I send you forth as sheep in the midst of wolves: be ye therefore wise as serpents, and harmless as doves.

19 But beware of men: for they will deliver you up to councils, and in their synagogues they will scourge you;

20 Yea and before governors and kings shall ye be brought for my sake, for a testimony to them and to the Gentiles.

21 But when they deliver you up, be not anxious how or what ye shall speak: for it shall be given you in that hour what ye shall speak.

22 For it is not ye that speak, but the Spirit of your Father that speaketh in you.

23 And brother shall deliver up brother to death, and the father his child: and children shall rise up against parents, and cause them to be put to death.

24 And ye shall be hated of all men for my name's sake: but he that endureth to the end, the same shall be saved.

25 But when they persecute you in this city, flee into the next: for verily I say unto you, Ye shall not have gone through the cities of Israel, till the Son of man be come.

26 A disciple is not above his master, nor a servant above his lord.

27 It is enough for the disciple that he be as his master, and the servant as his lord. If they have called the master of the house Beelzebub, how much more *shall they call* them of his household!

28 Fear them not therefore: for there is nothing covered, that shall not be revealed; and hid, that shall not be known.

29 What I tell you in the darkness, speak ye in the light; and what ye hear in the ear, proclaim upon the housetops.

30 And be not afraid of them which kill the body, but are not able to kill the soul; but rather fear him which is able to destroy both soul and body in hell.

31 Are not two sparrows sold for a farthing? and not one of them shall fall on the ground without your Father:

32 But the very hairs of your head are all numbered.

33 Fear not therefore; ye are of more value than many sparrows.

34 Every one therefore who shall confess me before men, him will I also confess before my Father which is in heaven.

35 But whosoever shall deny me before men, him will I also deny before my Father which is in heaven.

36 Think not that I came to send peace on the earth: I came not to send peace, but a sword.

37 For I came to set a man at variance against his father, and the daughter against her mother, and the daughter in law against her mother in law:

38 And a man's foes *shall be* they of his own household.

39 He that loveth father or mother more than me is not worthy of me; and he that loveth son or daughter more than me is not worthy of me.

40 And he that doth not take his cross and follow after me, is not worthy of me.

41 He that findeth his life shall lose it; and he that loseth his life for my sake shall find it.

42 He that receiveth you receiveth me, and he that receiveth me receiveth him that sent me.

43 He that receiveth a prophet in the name of a prophet shall receive a prophet's reward; and he that receiveth a righteous man in the name of a righteous man shall receive a righteous man's reward.

44 And whosoever shall give to drink unto one of

JOHN THE BAPTIST BEHEADED.

these little ones a cup of cold water only, in the name of a disciple, verily I say unto you, he shall in no wise lose his reward.

45 And it came to pass, when Jesus had made an end of commanding his twelve disciples, he departed thence to teach and to preach in their cities.

46 And they departed, and went throughout the villages, preaching the gospel, and healing everywhere.

47 And they cast out many devils, and anointed with oil many that were sick, and healed them.

### THE BAPTIST BEHEADED.

48 At that season Herod the tetrarch heard the report concerning Jesus, for his name had become known.

49 And he said, John the Baptist is risen from the dead, and therefore do these powers work in him.

50 But others said, It is Elijah. And others said, *It is* a prophet, *even* as one of the prophets.

51 But Herod said, John, whom I beheaded, he is risen.

52 For Herod had sent forth and laid hold upon John, and bound him in prison for the sake of Herodias. And when he would have put him to death, he feared the multitude, because they counted him as a prophet.

53 For John said unto Herod, It is not lawful for thee to have thy brother's wife.

54 And Herodias set herself against him, and desired to kill him; and she could not,

55 For Herod feared John, knowing that he was a righteous man and a holy, and kept him safe. And when he heard him, he was much perplexed; and he heard him gladly.

56 And when a convenient day was come, that Herod on his birthday made a supper to his lords, and the high captains, and the chief men' of Galilee;

57 And when the daughter of Herodias herself came in

and danced, she pleased Herod and them that sat at meat with him; and the king said unto the damsel, Ask of me whatsoever thou wilt, and I will give it thee.

58 And he sware unto her, Whatsoever thou shalt ask of me, I will give it thee, unto the half of my kingdom.

59 And she went out, and said unto her mother, What shall I ask? And she said, The head of John the Baptist.

60 And she came in straightway with haste unto the king, and asked, saying, I will that thou forthwith give me in a charger the head of John the Baptist.

61 And the king was exceeding sorry; but for the sake of his oaths, and of them that sat at meat, he would not reject her.

March, A. D. 29.

62 And straightway the king sent forth a soldier of his guard, and commanded to bring his head: and he went and beheaded John in prison,

63 And brought his head in a charger, and gave it to the damsel; and the damsel gave it to her mother.

64 And when his disciples heard *thereof*, they came and took up his corpse, and laid it in a tomb, and went and told Jesus.

## CHAPTER XXIV.

### THE FIVE THOUSAND FED.

AND the apostles gathered themselves together unto Jesus; and they told him all things, whatsoever they had done, and whatsoever they had taught.

2 And he saith unto them, Come ye yourselves apart into a desert place, and rest a while. For there were many coming and going, and they had no leisure so much as to eat.

3 And they went away in the boat to the other side of the sea of Galilee, which is *the sea* of Tiberias, to a desert place apart.

4 And *the people* saw them going, and many knew *them*,

THE FUNERAL OF JOHN THE BAPTIST.

and they ran there together on foot from all the cities, and outwent them.

5 Because they beheld the signs which he did on them that were sick.

6 And he came forth and saw a great multitude, and he had compassion on them, because they were as sheep not having a shepherd:

7 And he welcomed them, and he spake to them of the kingdom of God, and them that had need of healing he healed.

8 And the day began to wear away; and the twelve came, and said unto him, Send the multitude away, that they may go into the villages and country round about, and lodge, and get victuals: for we are here in a desert place.

9 But he answered and said, unto them, Give ye them to eat. And they say unto him, Shall we go and buy two hundred pennyworth of bread, and give them to eat?

10 Jesus saith unto Philip, Whence are we to buy bread, that these may eat?

11 And this he said to prove him: for he himself knew what he would do.

12 Philip answered him, Two hundred pennyworth of bread is not sufficient for them, that every one may take a little.

13 And he saith unto them, How many loaves have ye? go *and* see.

14 One of his disciples, Andrew, Simon Peter's brother, saith unto him, There is a lad here, which hath five barley loaves, and two fishes: but what are these among so many?

15 Jesus said, Make the people sit down. Now there was much grass in the place.

16 And they sat down in ranks, by hundreds, and by fifties.

April, A D. 29.

17 And Jesus took the five loaves and the two fishes, and looking up to heaven, he blessed and brake the loaves;

and he gave to the disciples to set before them; and the two fishes divided he among them all.

18 And they did all eat, and were filled.

19 And when they were filled, he saith unto his disciples, Gather up the broken pieces which remain over, that nothing be lost.

20 And they took up broken pieces, twelve basketfuls, and also of the fishes.

21 And they that did eat were about five thousand men, beside women and children.

22 When therefore the people saw the sign which he did, they said, This is of truth the prophet that cometh into the world.

23 Jesus therefore perceiving that they were about to come and take him by force, to make him king,

24 Straightway he constrained his disciples to enter into the boat, and to go before *him* unto the other side to Bethsaida, while he himself sendeth the multitude away.

25 And after he had sent the multitudes away, he went up into the mountain apart to pray: and when even was come, he was there alone.

26 And the sea was rising by reason of a great wind that blew.

27 But the boat was now in the midst of the sea, distressed by the waves, for the wind was contrary.

JESUS WALKS ON THE SEA.
April, A. D. 29.

28 And seeing them distressed in rowing, for the wind was contrary unto them, about the fourth watch of the night he cometh unto them, walking on the sea; and he would have passed by them:

29 But they, when they saw him walking on the sea, supposed that it was an apparition, and cried out:

30 For they all saw him and were troubled. But he

"LORD, SAVE ME."

straightway spake with them, and saith unto them, Be of good cheer: it is I; be not afraid.

31 And Peter answered him and said, Lord, if it be thou, bid me come unto thee upon the waters. And he said, Come.

32 And Peter went down from the boat, and walked upon the waters, to come to Jesus.

33 But when he saw the wind, he was afraid; and beginning to sink, he cried out, saying, Lord, save me.

34 And immediately Jesus stretched forth his hand, and took hold of him, and saith unto him, O thou of little faith, wherefore didst thou doubt?

35 And when they were gone up into the boat, the wind ceased, and they were sore amazed in themselves;

36 For they understood not concerning the loaves, but their heart was hardened.

37 And straightway the boat was at the land whither they were going.

38 And they that were in the boat worshipped him, saying, Of a truth thou art the Son of God.

39 They came to the land Gennesaret, and moored to the shore.

40 And when they were come out of the boat, straightway *the people* knew him.

41 And ran round about that whole region, and began to carry about on their beds those that were sick, where they heard he was.

42 And wheresoever he entered, into villages, or into cities, or into the country, they laid the sick in the marketplaces, and besought him that they might touch if it were but the border of his garment: and as many as touched him were made whole.

THE BREAD OF LIFE.

43 On the morrow the multitude which stood on the other side of the sea saw

that there was none other boat there, save one, and that Jesus entered not with his disciples into the boat, but *that* his disciples went away alone.

44 (Howbeit there c a m e boats from Tiberias nigh unto the place where they ate the bread after the Lord had given thanks):

45 When the multitude therefore saw that Jesus was not there, neither his disciples, they themselves got into the boats, and came to Capernaum, seeking Jesus.

46 And when they found him on the other side of the sea, they said unto him, Rabbi, when camest thou hither?

47 Jesus answered them and said, Verily, verily, I say unto you, Ye seek me, not because ye saw signs, but because ye ate of the loaves, and were filled.

48 Work not for the meat which perisheth, but for the meat which abideth unto eternal life, which the Son of man shall give unto you: for him the Father, *even* God, hath sealed.

49 They said therefore unto him, What must we do, that we may work the works of God?

50 Jesus answered and said unto them, This is the work of God, that ye believe on him whom he hath sent.

## CHAPTER XXV.

THEY said therefore unto him, What then doest thou for a sign, that we may see, and believe thee? what workest thou?

2 Our fathers ate the manna in the wilderness; as it is written, He gave them bread out of heaven to eat.

3 Jesus therefore said unto them, Verily, verily, I say unto you, It was not Moses that gave you the bread out of heaven; but my Father giveth you the true bread out of heaven.

4 For the bread of God is that which cometh down out

"Him that Cometh to Me I Will in No Wise Cast Out."

of heaven, and giveth life unto the world.

5 They said therefore unto him, Lord, evermore give us this bread.

6 Jesus said unto them, I am the bread of life: he that cometh to me shall not hunger, and he that believeth on me shall never thirst.

7 But I said unto you, that ye have seen me, and yet believe not.

8 All that which the Father giveth me shall come unto me; and him that cometh to me I will in no wise cast out.

9 For I am come down from heaven, not to do mine own will, but the will of him that sent me.

10 And this is the will of him that sent me, that of all that which he hath given me I should lose nothing, but should raise it up at the last day.

11 For this is the will of my Father, that every one that beholdeth the Son, and believeth on him, should have eternal life; and I will raise him up at the last day.

12 The Jews therefore murmured concerning him, because he said, I am the bread which came down out of heaven.

13 And they said, Is not this Jesus, the son of Joseph, whose father and mother we know? how doth he now say, I am come down out of heaven?

14 Jesus answered and said unto them, Murmur not among yourselves.

15 No man can come to me, except the Father which sent me draw him: and I will raise him up in the last day.

16 It is written in the prophets, And they shall all be taught of God. Every one that hath heard from the Father, and hath learned, cometh unto me.

17 Not that any man hath seen the Father, save he which is from God, he hath seen the Father.

18 Verily, verily, I say

unto you, He that believeth hath eternal life.

19 I am the bread of life.

20 Your fathers did eat the manna in the wilderness, and they died.

21 This is the bread which cometh down out of heaven, that a man may eat thereof, and not die.

22 I am the living bread which came down out of heaven: if any man eat of this bread, he shall live for ever: yea and the bread which I will give is my flesh, for the life of the world.

23 The Jews therefore strove one with another, saying, How can this man give us his flesh to eat?

24 Jesus therefore said unto them, Verily, verily, I say unto you, Except ye eat the flesh of the Son of man and drink his blood, ye have not life in yourselves.

25 He that eateth my flesh and drinketh my blood hath eternal life; and I will raise him up at the last day.

26 For my flesh is meat indeed, and my blood is drink indeed.

27 He that eateth my flesh and drinketh my blood abideth in me, and I in him.

28 As the living Father sent me, and I live because of the Father; so he that eateth me, he also shall live because of me.

29 This is the bread which came down out of heaven: not as the fathers did eat, and died: he that eateth this bread shall live for ever.

30 These things said he in the synagogue, as he taught in Capernaum.

31 Many therefore of his disciples, when they heard *this*, said, This is a hard saying; who can hear it?

32 But Jesus knowing in himself that his disciples murmured at this, said unto them, Doth this cause you to stumble?

33 *What* then if ye should behold the Son of man ascending where he was before?

34 It is the spirit that

THE BREAD OF LIFE SERMON AT CAPERNAUM.

quickeneth; the flesh profiteth nothing: the words that I have spoken unto you are spirit, and are life.

35 But there are some of you that believe not. For Jesus knew from the beginning who they were that believed not, and who it was that should betray him.

36 And he said, For this cause have I said unto you, that no man can come unto me, except it be given unto him of the Father.

37 Upon this many of his disciples went back, and walked no more with him.

38 Jesus said therefore unto the twelve, Would ye also go away?

39 Simon Peter answered him, Lord, to whom shall we go? thou hast the words of eternal life.

40 And we have believed and know that thou art the Holy One of God.

41 Jesus answered them. Did not I choose you the twelve, and one of you is a devil?

42 Now he spake of Judas *the son* of Simon Iscariot, for he it was that should betray him, *being* one of the twelve.

## CHAPTER XXVI.

### THE TRADITIONS OF MEN.

AND there are gathered together unto him the Pharisees, and certain of the scribes, which had come from Jerusalem,

2 And had seen that some of his disciples ate their bread with defiled, that is, unwashen, hands.

3 For the Pharisees, and all the Jews, except they wash their hands diligently, eat not, holding the tradition of the elders:

4 And *when they come* from the marketplace, except they wash themselves, they eat not; and many other things there be, which they have received to hold, washings of cups, and pots, and brasen vessels.

5 And the Pharisees and scribes ask him, Why walk not thy disciples according

to the tradition of the elders, but eat their bread with defiled hands?

6 And he answered and said unto them, Why do ye also transgress the commandment of God because of your tradition?

7 Full well do ye reject the commandment of God, that ye may keep your tradition.

8 For Moses said, Honour thy father and thy mother; and, He that speaketh evil of father or mother, let him die the death: but ye say,

9 If a man shall say to his father or his mother, That wherewith thou mightest have been profited by me is Corban, that is to say, Given *to God;*

10 Ye no longer suffer him to do aught for his father or his mother; making void the word of God by your tradition, which ye have delivered: and many such like things ye do.

11 And he said unto them, Well did Isaiah prophesy of you hypocrites, as it is written,

This people honoureth me with their lips,

But their heart is far from me.

But in vain do they worship me,

12 Teaching *as their* doctrines the precepts of men.

13 Ye leave the commandment of God, and hold fast the tradition of men.

14 And he called to him the multitude again, and said unto them, Hear me all of you, and understand:

15 there is nothing from without the man, that going into him can defile him: but the things which proceed out of the man are those that defile the man.

16 And when he was entered into the house from the multitude,

17 Then came the disciples, and said unto him, Knowest thou that the Pharisees were offended, when they heard this saying?

18 But he answered and

JESUS AND THE SYROPHENICIAN WOMAN.

said, Every plant which my heavenly Father planted not, shall be rooted up.

19 Let them alone: they are blind guides. And if the blind guide the blind, both shall fall into a pit.

20 And Peter answered and said unto him, Declare unto us the parable.

21 And he said, Are ye also even yet without understanding?

22 Perceive ye not, that whatsoever from w i t h o u t goeth into the man, *it* cannot defile him;

23 Because it goeth not into his heart, but into his belly, and goeth out into the draught? *This he said,* making all meats clean.

24 But the things which proceed out of the mouth come forth out of the heart; and they defile the man.

25 For from within, out of the heart of men, evil thoughts proceed,

26 Fornications, t h e f t s, murders, adulteries, covetings, wickednesses, deceit, lasciviousness, and evil eye, railing, pride, foolishness:

27 These are the things which defile the man: but to eat with unwashen hands defileth not the man.

## THE SYROPHŒNICIAN WOMAN.

May, A. D. 29.

28 And from thence Jesus arose, and went away into the borders of Tyre and Sidon. And he entered into a house, and would have no man know it: and he could not be hid.

29 But s t r a i g h t w a y a woman, whose little daughter had an unclean spirit, having heard of him, came and fell down at his feet.

30 The woman was a Greek, a Syrophœnician by race; a Canaanitish woman.

31 And cried, saying, Have mercy on me, O Lord, thou son of David; my daughter is grievously vexed with a devil.

32 But he answered her not a word. And his disciples came and besought him,

saying, Send her away; for she crieth after us.

33 But he answered and said, I was not sent but unto the lost sheep of the house of Israel.

34 But she came and worshipped him, saying, Lord, help me.

35 And he said unto her, Let the children first be filled: for it is not meet to take the children's bread and cast it to the dogs.

36 But she answered and saith unto him, Yea, Lord: even the dogs under the table eat of the children's crumbs.

37 Then Jesus answered and said unto her, O woman, great is thy faith: be it done unto thee even as thou wilt.

38 For this saying go thy way; the devil is gone out of thy daughter.

39 And she went away unto her house, and found the child laid upon the bed, and the devil gone out.

## CHAPTER XXVII.
### SPEECH GIVEN.
#### June, A. D. 29.

AND again he went out from the borders of Tyre, and came through Sidon unto the sea of Galilee, through the midst of the borders of Decapolis.

2 And they bring unto him one that was deaf, and had an impediment in his speech; and they beseech him to lay his hand upon him.

3 And he took him aside from the multitude privately, and put his fingers into his ears, and he spat, and touched his tongue;

4 And looking up to heaven, he sighed, and saith unto him, Ephphatha, that is, Be opened.

5 And his ears were opened, and the bond of his tongue was loosed, and he spake plain.

6 And he charged them that they should tell no man: but the more he charged them, so much the more a great deal they published it.

"And Looking up to Heaven He Sighed and Saith Unto Him Ephphatha."

7 And they were beyond measure astonished, saying, He hath done all things well: he maketh even the deaf to hear, and the dumb to speak.

8 And Jesus departed thence, and came nigh unto the sea of Galilee; and he went up into the mountain, and sat there.

### THE LAME AND BLIND AND MAIMED.

9 And there came unto him great multitudes, having with them the lame, blind, dumb, maimed, and many others, and they cast them down at his feet; and he healed them:

10 Insomuch that the multitude wondered, when they saw the dumb speaking, the maimed whole, and the lame walking, and the blind seeing: and they glorified the God of Israel.

### THE FOUR THOUSAND FED.

11 In those days, when there was again a great multitude, and they had nothing to eat, he called unto him his disciples, and saith unto them,

12 I have compassion on the multitude, because they continue with me now three days, and have nothing to eat:

13 And if I send them away fasting to their home, they will faint in the way; and some of them are come from far.

14 And his disciples answered him, Whence shall one be able to fill these men with bread here in a desert place?

15 And he asked them, How many loaves have ye?

16 And they said, seven. And he commandeth the multitude to sit down on the ground: and he took the seven loaves, and having given thanks, he brake, and gave to his disciples, to set before them; and they set them before the multitude.

17 And they had a few small fishes: and having blessed them, he commanded to set these also before them.

18 And they did eat, and

were filled: and they took up, of broken pieces that remained over, seven baskets.

19 And they that did eat were four thousand men, beside women and children. And he sent them away.

20 And straightway he entered into the boat with his disciples, and came into the borders of Magadan, into the parts of Dalmanutha.

21 And the Pharisees came forth, and began to question with him, seeking of him a sign from heaven, tempting him.

22 And he sighed deeply in his spirit, and said unto them, When it is evening, ye say, *It will be* fair weather: for the heaven is red.

23 And in the morning, *It will be* foul weather to-day: for the heaven is red and lowering. Ye know how to discern the face of the heaven; but ye cannot *discern* the signs of the times.

24 An evil and adulterous generation seeketh after a sign; and there shall no sign be given unto it, but the sign of Jonah.

25 And he left them, and again entering into *the boat* departed to the other side.

26 And they forgot to take bread; and they had not in the boat with them more than one loaf.

27 And he charged them, saying, Take heed, beware of the leaven of the Pharisees and the leaven of Herod.

28 And they r e a s o n e d among themselves, saying, We took no bread.

29 And Jesus perceiving it said, O ye of little faith, why reason ye among yourselves, because ye have no bread? do ye not yet perceive, neither understand? have ye your heart hardened?

30 Having eyes, see ye not? and having ears, hear ye not?

31 Do ye not yet perceive, neither remember the five loaves of the five thousand, and how many baskets ye took up?

32 When I brake the five loaves among the five thousand, how many baskets full of broken pieces took ye up? They say unto him, Twelve.

33 And when the seven among the four thousand, how many basketfuls of broken pieces took ye up? And they say unto him, Seven.

34 And he said unto them, Do ye not yet understand?

35 How is it that ye do not perceive that I spake not to you concerning bread?

36 Beware of the leaven of the Pharisees and Sadducees.

37 Then understood they how that he bade them not beware of the leaven of bread, but of the teaching of the Pharisees and Sadducees.

## CHAPTER XXVIII.
### June, A. D. 29.

AND they come unto Bethsaida. And they bring to him a blind man, and beseech him to touch him.

2 And he took hold of the blind man by the hand, and brought him out of the village; and when he had spit on his eyes, and laid his hands upon him, he asked him, Seest thou aught?

3 And he looked up, and said, I see men; for I behold *them* as trees, walking.

4 Then again he laid his hands upon his eyes; and he looked steadfastly, and was restored, and saw all things clearly.

5 And he sent him away to his home, saying, Do not even enter into the village.

6 And Jesus went forth, and his disciples, into the villages of Cæsarea Philippi:

### WHO SAY YE THAT I AM?

7 And it came to pass, as he was praying alone, the disciples were with him: and he asked them, saying, Who do men say that the Son of man is?

8 Who do the multitudes say that I am?

9 And they said, some *say*

John the Baptist; some, Elijah: and others, Jeremiah, or one of the old prophets risen again.

10 He saith unto them, But who say ye that I am?

11 And Simon Peter answered and said, Thou art the Christ, the Son of the living God.

12 And Jesus answered and said unto him, Blessed art thou, Simon Bar-Jonah: for flesh and blood hath not revealed it unto thee, but my Father which is in heaven.

13 And I also say unto thee, that thou art Peter, and upon this rock I will build my church; and the gates of Hades shall not prevail against it.

14 I will give unto thee the keys of the kingdom of h e a v e n : and whatsoever thou shalt bind on earth shall be bound in heaven. and whatsoever thou shalt loose on earth shall be loosed in heaven.

15 Then charged he the disciples that they should tell no man that he was the Christ.

### JESUS PREDICTS HIS DEATH.
#### Summer, A. D. 29.

16 From that time began Jesus to shew unto his disciples, how that he must go unto Jerusalem, and suffer many things of the elders and chief priests and scribes, and be killed, and after three days rise again.

17 And he spake the saying openly.

18 And Peter took him, and began to rebuke him, saying, Be it far from thee, Lord: this shall never be unto thee.

19 But he turning about, and seeing his disciples, rebuked Peter, and saith, Thou art a stumbling-block unto me: Get thee behind me, Satan: for thou mindest not the things of God, but the things of men.

20 And he called unto him the multitude with his disciples, and said unto them, If any man would come

" BLESSED ART THOU SIMON."

after me, let him deny himself, and take up his cross, and follow me.

21 For whosoever would save his life shall lose it; and whosoever shall lose his life for my sake and the gospel's shall save it.

22 For what shall a man be profited, if he shall gain the whole world, and forfeit his life? or what shall a man give in exchange for his life?

23 For the Son of man shall come in the glory of his Father with his angels; and then shall he render unto every man according to his deeds.

24 Whosoever shall be ashamed of me and of my words in this adulterous and sinful generation, the Son of man also shall be ashamed of him, when he cometh in the glory of his Father with the holy angels.

25 And verily I say unto you, There be some here of them that stand *by* which shall in no wise taste of death, till they see the king-dom of God come with power.

## CHAPTER XXIX.
### THE TRANSFIGURATION.
#### Summer, A. D. 29.

AND after six days Jesus taketh with him Peter, and James, and John his brother, and bringeth them up into a high mountain apart to pray.

2 And as he was praying, he was transfigured before them:

3 The fashion of his countenance was altered, and his raiment *became* white *and* dazzling, so as no fuller on earth can whiten them.

4 And behold, there talked with him two men, which were Moses and Elijah; who appeared in glory, and spake of his decease which he was about to accomplish at Jerusalem.

5 Now Peter and they that were with him were heavy with sleep: but when they were fully awake, they saw his glory, and the two men that stood with him.

6 And it came to pass, as they were parting from him, Peter said unto Jesus, Master, it is good for us to be here: and let us make three tabernacles; one for thee, and one for Moses, and one for Elijah: not knowing what he said.

7 For he wist not what to answer; for they became sore afraid.

8 And while he said these things, there came a cloud, and overshadowed them: and they feared as they entered into the cloud.

9 And a voice came out of the cloud, saying,

This is my beloved Son, in whom I am well pleased; hear ye him.

10 And when the disciples heard it, they fell on their face, and were sore afraid.

11 And Jesus came and touched then and said, Arise, and be not afraid.

12 And suddenly looking round about, they saw no one any more, save Jesus only with themselves.

13 And as they were coming down from the mountain, Jesus commanded them, saying, Tell the vision to no man, until the Son of man be risen from the dead.

14 And they kept the saying, questioning among themselves what the rising again from the dead should mean.

15 And his disciples asked him, saying, Why then say the scribes that Elijah must first come?

16 And he said unto them, Elijah indeed cometh first, and restoreth all things; and how is it written of the Son of man, that he should suffer many things and be set at nought?

17 But I say unto you, that Elijah is come already, and they knew him not, but did unto him whatsoever they listed. Even so shall the Son of man also suffer of them.

18 Then understood the disciples that he spake unto them of John the Baptist.

THE EPILEPTIC CURED.

19 And it came to pass, on the next day, when they were come down from the mountain,

20 And came to the disciples, they saw a great multitude about them, and scribes questioning with them.

21 And straightway all the multitude, when they saw him, were greatly amazed, and running to him saluted him.

22 And he asked them, What question ye with them?

Summer, A. D. 29.

23 And behold, a man from the multitude came kneeling to him and cried, saying, Master, I beseech thee to look upon my son; for he is mine only child:

24 Lord, have mercy on my son: for he is epileptic, and suffereth grievously: for oft-times he falleth into the fire, and oft-times into the water.

25 And behold, a spirit taketh him, and he suddenly crieth out; and it teareth him that he foameth, and it hardly departeth from him, bruising him sorely.

26 And I besought thy disciples to cast it out; and they could not.

27 And Jesus answered and said, O faithless and perverse generation, how long shall I be with you? how long shall I bear with you? bring him hither to me.

28 And they brought him unto him: and when he saw him, straightway the spirit tare him grievously; and he fell on the ground, and wallowed foaming.

29 And he asked his father How long time is it since this hath come unto him? And he said, From a child.

30 And oft-times it hath cast him both into the fire and into the waters, to destroy him: but if thou canst do anything, have compassion on us, and help us.

31 And Jesus said unto him, · If thou canst! All things are possible to him that believeth.

32 Straightway the father of the child cried out, and said, I believe; help thou mine unbelief.

33 And when Jesus saw that a multitude came running together, he rebuked the unclean spirit, saying unto him, Thou dumb and deaf spirit, I command thee, come out of him, and enter no more into him.

34 And having cried out, and torn him much, he came out: and *the child* became as one dead; insomuch that the more part said, he is dead.

35 But Jesus took him by the hand, and raised him up; and he arose and the boy was cured from that hour.

36 And they were all astonished at the majesty of God.

37 Then came the disciples to Jesus apart, and said, Why could not we cast it out?

38 And he saith unto them, Because of your little faith:

39 For verily I say unto you, If ye have faith as a grain of mustard seed, ye shall say unto this mountain, Remove hence to yonder place; and it shall remove; and nothing shall be impossible unto you.

40 And he said unto them, this kind can come out by nothing, save by prayer.

## CHAPTER XXX.

Autumn, A. D. 29.

AND they went forth from thence, and passed through Galilee; and he would not that any man should know it.

2 He would not walk in Judæa, because the Jews sought to kill him.

3 And while they abode in Galilee, and while all were marveling at all the things which he did, he said unto his disciples,

4 Let these words sink into your ears:

5 The Son of man shall be delivered up into the hands of men;

6 And they shall kill him;

and when he is killed, after three days he shall rise again.

7 And they were exceeding sorry:

8 But they understood not this saying, and it was concealed from them, that they should not perceive it: and they were afraid to ask him about this saying.

### THE TRIBUTE MONEY.

9 And when they were come to Capernaum, they that received the half-shekel came to Peter, and said, Doth not your master pay the half-shekel? He saith, Yea.

10 And when he came into the house, Jesus spake first to him, saying, What thinkest thou, Simon? the kings of the earth, from whom do they receive toll or tribute? from their sons, or from strangers?

11 And when he said, From strangers, Jesus said unto him, Therefore the sons are free.

12 But, lest we cause them to stumble, go thou to the sea, and cast a hook, and take up the fish that first cometh up; and when thou hast opened his mouth, thou shalt find a shekel: that take, and give unto them for me and thee.

13 And when he was in the house he asked them, What were ye reasoning in the way?

14 But they held their peace: for they had disputed one with another in the way, who *was* the greatest.

15 And he sat down, and called the twelve; and he saith unto them, if any man would be first, he shall be last of all, and minister of all.

16 And he took a little child, and set him in the midst of them; and taking him in his arms, he said unto them,

17 Verily I say unto you, Except ye turn, and become as little children, ye shall in no wise enter into the kingdom of heaven.

18 Whosoever therefore

shall humble himself as this little child, the same is the greatest in the kingdom of heaven.

19 Whosoever shall receive one of such little children in my name, receiveth me; and whosoever shall receive me receiveth him that sent me: for he that is least among you all, the same is great.

20 John said unto him, Master, we saw one casting out devils in thy name: and we forbade him, because he followed not us.

21 But Jesus said, Forbid him not: for there is no man which shall do a mighty work in my name, and be able quickly to speak evil of me.

22 For he that is not against us is for us.

23 For whosover shall give you a cup of water to drink, because ye are Christ's, verily I say unto you, he shall in no wise lose his reward.

24 And whosoever shall cause one of these little ones that believe on me to stumble, it were better for him if a great millstone were hanged about his neck, and he were cast into the sea.

25 Woe unto the world because of occasions of stumbling! for it must needs be that the occasions come; but woe to that man through whom the occasion cometh!

26 And if thy hand cause thee to stumble, cut it off:

27 It is good for thee to enter into life maimed, rather than having thy two hands to go into hell, into the unquenchable fire.

28 And if thy foot cause thee to stumble, cut it off:

29 It is good for thee to enter into life halt, rather than having thy two feet to be cast into hell.

30 And if thine eye cause thee to stumble, cast it out:

31 It is good for thee to enter into the kingdom of God with one eye, rather than having two eyes to be cast into hell;

"WOE UNTO THOSE WHO CAUSE THESE LITTLE ONES TO STUMBLE"

32 Where their worm dieth not, and the fire is not quenched.

33 For every one shall be salted with fire.

34 Salt is good: but if the salt have lost its saltness, wherewith will ye season it? Have salt in yourselves, and be at peace one with another.

## CHAPTER XXXI.

SEE that ye despise not one of these little ones; for I say unto you, that in heaven their angels do always behold the face of my Father which is in heaven.

2 How think ye? if any man have a hundred sheep, and one of them be gone astray, doth he not leave the ninety and nine, and go unto the mountains, and seek that which goeth astray?

3 And if so be that he find it, verily I say unto you, he rejoiceth over it more than over the ninety and nine which have not gone astray.

4 Even so it is not the will of your Father which is in heaven, that one of these little ones should perish.

5 For the Son of man came to seek and to save that which was lost.

6 And if thy brother sin against thee go shew him his fault between thee and him alone: if he hear thee, thou hast gained thy brother.

7 But if he hear *thee* not, take with thee one or two more, that at the mouth of two witnesses or three every word may be established.

8 And if he refuse to hear them, tell it unto the church: and if he refuse to hear the church also, let him be unto thee as the Gentile and the publican.

9 Verily I say unto you, What things soever ye shall bind on earth shall be bound in heaven: and what things soever ye shall loose on earth shall be loosed in heaven.

10 Again I say unto you, that if two of you shall agree on earth as touching anything that they shall ask, it

shall be done for them of my Father which is in heaven.

11 For where two or three are gathered together in my name, there am I in the midst of them.

12 Then came Peter, and said to him, Lord, how oft shall my brother sin against me, and I forgive him? until seven times?

13 Jesus saith unto him, I say not unto thee, Until seven times; but, Until seventy times seven.

14 Therefore is the kingdom of heaven likened unto a certain king, which would make a reckoning with his servants.

15 And when he had begun to reckon, one was brought unto him, which owed him ten thousand talents.

16 But forasmuch as he had not *wherewith* to pay, his lord commanded him to be sold, and his wife, and children, and all that he had, and payment to be made.

17 The servant therefore fell down and worshipped him, saying, Lord, have patience with me, and I will pay thee all.

18 And the lord of that servant, being moved with compassion, released him, and forgave him the debt.

19 But that servant went out, and found one of his fellow-servants, which owed him a hundred pence: and he laid hold on him, and took *him* by the throat, saying, Pay what thou owest.

20 So his fellow-servant fell down and besought him, saying, Have patience with me, and I will pay thee.

21 And he would not: but went and cast him into prison, till he should pay that which was due.

22 So when his fellow-servants saw what was done, they were exceeding sorry, and came and told unto their lord all that was done.

23 Then his lord called him unto him, and saith to him, Thou wicked servant, I forgave thee all that debt,

"PEACE BE TO THIS HOUSE."

because thou besoughtest me:

24 Shouldest not thou also have had mercy on thy fellow-servant, even as I had mercy on thee?

25 And his lord was wroth, and delivered him to the tormentors, till he should pay all that was due.

26 So shall also my heavenly Father do unto you, if ye forgive not every one his brother from your hearts.

## CHAPTER XXXII.

### THE SEVENTY SENT OUT.

NOW after these things the Lord appointed seventy others and sent them two and two before his face into every city and place, whither he himself was about to come.

2 And he said unto them, The harvest is plenteous, but the labourers are few: pray ye therefore the Lord of the harvest, that he send forth labourers into his harvest.

3 Go your ways: behold, I send you forth as lambs in the midst of wolves.

4 Carry no purse, no wallet, no shoes: and salute no man on the way.

5 And into whatsoever house ye shall enter, first say, Peace *be* to this house.

6 And if a son of peace be there, your peace shall rest upon him: but if not, it shall turn to you again.

7 And in that same house remain, eating and drinking such things as they give: for the labourer is worthy of his hire. Go not from house to house.

8 And into whatsoever city ye enter, and they receive you, eat such things as are set before you:

9 And heal the sick that are therein, and say unto them, The kingdom of God is come nigh unto you.

10 But into whatsoever city ye shall enter, and they receive you not, go out into the streets thereof and say,

11 Even the dust from your city, that cleaveth to

our feet, we do wipe off against you: howbeit know this, that the kingdom of God is come nigh.

12 I say unto you, It shall be more tolerable in that day for Sodom, than for that city.

13 Woe unto thee, Chorazin! woe unto thee, Bethsaida! for if the mighty works had been done in Tyre and Sidon, which were done in you, they would have repented long ago, sitting in sackcloth and ashes.

14 Howbeit it shall be more tolerable for Tyre and Sidon in the judgement, than for you.

15 And thou, Capernaum, shalt thou be exalted unto heaven? thou shalt be brought down unto Hades.

16 He that heareth you heareth me; and he that rejecteth you rejecteth me; and he that rejecteth me rejecteth him that sent me.

17 And the seventy returned with joy, saying, Lord, even the devils are subject unto us in thy name.

18 And he said unto them, I beheld Satan fallen as lightning from heaven.

19 Behold, I have given you authority to tread upon serpents and scorpions, and over all the power of the enemy: and nothing shall in any wise hurt you.

20 Howbeit in this rejoice not, that the spirits are subject unto you; but rejoice that your names are written in heaven.

21 In that same hour Jesus rejoiced in the Holy Spirit, and said, I thank thee, O Father, Lord of heaven and earth, that thou didst hide these things from the wise and understanding, and didst reveal them unto babes: yea, Father; for so it was well-pleasing in thy sight.

22 All things have been delivered unto me of my Father: and no one knoweth who the Son is save the Father; and who the Father is, save the Son, and he to whomsoever the Son willeth to reveal *him*.

"Satan Falling as Lightning from Heaven."

23 And turning to the disciples, he said privately, Blessed *are* the eyes which see the things that ye see:

24 For I say unto you, that many prophets and kings desired to see the things which ye see, and saw them not; and to hear the things which ye hear, and heard them not.

25 Now the feast of the Jews, the feast of tabernacles, was at hand.

26 His brethren therefore said unto him, Depart hence, and go into Judæa, that thy disciples also may behold thy works which thou doest.

27 For no man doeth anything in secret, and himself seeketh to be known openly. If thou doest these things, manifest t h y s e l f to the world.

28 For even his brethren did not believe on him.

29 Jesus therefore saith unto them, My time is not yet come; but your time is alway ready.

30 The world cannot hate you; but me it hateth, because I testify of it, that its works are evil.

31 Go ye up unto the feast: I go not up yet unto this feast; because my time is not yet fulfilled.

32 And having said these things unto them, he abode *still* in Galilee.

### STEADFASTLY GOES TO JERUSALEM.

33 And it came to pass, when the days were well-nigh come that he should be received up, he steadfastly set his face to go to Jerusalem,

34 And sent messengers before his face: and they went, and entered into a village of the Samaritans, to make ready for him.

35 And they did not receive him, because his face was *as though he were* going to Jerusalem.

36 And when his disciples James 'and John saw *this*, they said, Lord, wilt thou that we bid fire to come

down from heaven, and consume them?

37 But he turned, and rebuked them.

38 And they went to another village.

### THE TEN LEPERS.

39 And as he entered into a certain village, there met him ten men that were lepers, which stood afar off:

40 And they lifted up their voices, saying, Jesus, Master, have mercy on us.

41 And when he saw them, he said unto them, Go and shew yourselves unto the priests. And it came to pass as they went, they were cleansed.

42 And one of them, when he saw that he was healed, turned back, with a loud voice glorifying God;

43 And he fell upon his face at his feet, giving him thanks: and he was a Samaritan.

44 And Jesus answering said, Were not the ten cleansed? but where are the nine?

45 Were there none found that returned to give glory to God, save this stranger?

46 And he said unto him, Arise, and go thy way: thy faith hath made thee whole.

### THE GOOD SAMARITAN.

47 And behold, a certain lawyer stood up and tempted him, saying, Master, what shall I do to inherit eternal life?

48 And he said unto him, What is written in the law? how readest thou?

49 And he answering said, Thou shalt love the Lord thy God with all thy heart, and with all thy soul, and with all thy strength, and with all thy mind; and thy neighbour as thyself.

50 And he said unto him, Thou hast answered right: this do, and thou shalt live.

51 But he, desiring to justify himself, said unto Jesus, And who is my neighbour?

52 Jesus made answer and said, A certain man was go-

"The Good Samaritan."

ing down from Jerusalem to Jericho; and he fell among robbers, which both stripped him and beat him, and departed, leaving him half dead.

53 And by chance a certain priest was going down that way: and when he saw him, he passed by on the other side.

54 And in like manner a Levite also, when he came to the place, and saw him, passed by on the other side.

55 But a certain Samaritan, as he journeyed, came where he was: and when he saw him, he was moved with compassion,

56 And came to him, and bound up his wounds, pouring on *them* oil and wine; and he set him on his own beast, and brought him to an inn, and took care of him.

57 And on the morrow he took out two pence, and gave them to the host, and said, Take care of him; and whatsoever thou spendest more,

I, when I come back again, will repay thee.

58 Which of these three, thinkest thou, proved neighbour unto him that fell among the robbers?

59 And he said, He that shewed mercy on him. And Jesus said unto him, Go, and do thou likewise.

## CHAPTER XXXIII.
### THE LORD'S PRAYER.

AND it come to pass, as he was praying in a certain place, that when he ceased, one of his disciples said unto him, Lord, teach us to pray, even as John also taught his disciples.

2 And he said unto them, When ye pray, say, Father, Hallowed be thy name. Thy kingdom come.

3 Give us day by day our daily bread.

4 And forgive us our sins; for we ourselves also forgive every one that is indebted to us. ' And bring us not into temptation.

5 And he said unto them,

Which of you shall have a friend, and shall go unto him at midnight, and say to him, Friend, lend me three loaves;

6 For a friend of mine is come to me from a journey, and I have nothing to set before him;

7 And he from within shall answer and say, Trouble me not: the door is now shut, and my children are with me in bed; I cannot rise and give thee?

8 I say unto you, Though he will not rise and give him, because he is his friend, yet because of his importunity he will arise and give him as many as he needeth.

9 And I say unto you, Ask, and it shall be given you; seek, and ye shall find; knock and it shall be opened unto you.

10 For every one that asketh receiveth; and he that seeketh findeth; and to him that knocketh it shall be opened.

11 And of which of you that is a father shall his son ask a loaf, and he give him a stone? or a fish, and he for a fish give him a serpent?

12 Or *if* he shall ask an egg, will he give him a scorpion?

13 If ye then, being evil, know how to give good gifts unto your children, how much more shall *your* heavenly Father give the Holy Spirit to them that ask him?

14 Now as they went on their way, he entered into a certain village: and a certain woman named Martha received him into her house.

15 And she had a sister called Mary, which also sat at the Lord's feet, and heard his word.

16 But Martha was cumbered about much serving; and she came up to him, and said, Lord, dost thou not care that my sister did leave me to serve alone? bid her therefore that she help me.

17 But the Lord answered and said unto her, Martha, Martha, thou art anxious

JESUS AT THE HOUSE OF MARY AND MARTHA.

and troubled about many things:

18 But one thing is needful: for 'Mary hath chosen the good part, which shall not be taken away from her.

19 ¶ The Jews sought Jesus at the feast, and said, Where is he?

20 And there was much murmuring among the multitudes concerning him: some said, He is a good man; others said, Not so, but he leadeth the multitude astray.

21 Howbeit no man spake openly of him for fear of the Jews.

October, A. D. 29.

22 But when it was now the midst of the feast Jesus went up into the temple, and taught.

23 The Jews therefore marvelled, saying, How knoweth this man letters, having never learned?

24 Jesus therefore answered them, and said, My teaching is not mine, but his that sent me.

25 If any man willeth to do his will, he shall know of the teaching, whether it be of God, or *whether* I speak from myself.

26 He that speaketh from himself seeketh his own glory: but he that seeketh the glory of him that sent him, the same is true, and no unrighteousness is in him.

27 Did not Moses give you the law, and *yet* none of you doeth the law? Why seek ye to kill me?

28 The multitude answered, Thou hast a devil: who seeketh to kill thee?

29 Jesus answered and said unto them, I did one work, and ye all marvel.

30 For this cause hath Moses given you circumcision (not that it is of Moses but of the fathers); and on the sabbath ye circumcise a man.

31 If a man receiveth circumcision on the sabbath, that the law of Moses may not be broken; are ye wroth with me, because I made a

man every whit whole on the sabbath?

32 Judge not according to appearance, but judge righteous judgement.

33 Some therefore of them of Jerusalem said, Is not this he whom they seek to kill?

34 And lo, he speaketh openly, and they say nothing unto him. Can it be that the rulers indeed know that this is the Christ?

35 Howbeit we know this man whence he is: but when the Christ cometh, no one knoweth whence he is.

36 Jesus therefore cried in the temple, teaching and saying, Ye both know me, and know whence I am; and I am not come of myself, but he that sent me is true, whom ye know not.

37 I know him; because I am from him, and he sent me.

38 They sought therefore to take him: and no man laid his hand on him, because his hour was not yet come.

39 But of the multitude many believed on him; and they said, When the Christ shall come, will he do more signs than those which this man hath done?

40 The Pharisees heard the multitude murmuring these things concerning him; and the chief priests and the Pharisees sent officers to take him.

41 Jesus therefore said, Yet a little while am I with you, and I go unto him that sent me.

42 Ye shall seek me, and shall not find me: and where I am, ye cannot come.

43 The Jews therefore said among themselves, Whither will this man go that we shall not find him? will he go unto the Dispersion among the Greeks, and teach the Greeks?

44 What is this word that he said, Ye shall seek me, and shall not find me: and where I am, ye cannot come?

45 Now on the last day, the great *day* of the feast, Jesus stood and cried, say-

JESUS AT THE FEAST OF TABERNACLES.

ing, if any man thirst, let him come unto me, and drink.

46 He that believeth on me, as the scripture hath said, out of his belly shall flow rivers of living water.

47 But this spake he of the Spirit, which they that believed on him were to receive: for the Spirit was not yet *given*; because Jesus was not yet glorified.

48 *Some* of the multitude therefore, when they heard these words, said, This is of a truth the prophet.

49 Others said, This is the Christ. But s o m e said, What, doth the Christ come out of Galilee?

50 Hath not the scripture said that the Christ cometh of the seed of David, and from Bethlehem, the village where David was?

51 So there arose a division in the multitude because of him.

52 And s o m e of them would have taken him; but no man laid hands on him.

53 The officers therefore came to the chief priests and Pharisees; and they said unto them, Why did ye not bring him?

54 The officers answered, Never man so spake.

55 The Pharisees therefore answered them, Are ye also led astray?

56 Hath any of the rulers believed on him, or of the Pharisees?

57 But t h i s multitude which knoweth not the law are accursed.

58 Nicodemus saith unto them (he that came to him before, being one of them),

59 Doth our law judge a man, except it first hear from himself and know what he doeth?

60 They a n s w e r e d and said unto him, Art thou also of Galilee? Search, and see that out of Galilee ariseth no prophet.

### THE WOMAN TAKEN IN ADULTERY.

61 ‘[And they went every man unto his own house:

but Jesus went unto the mount of Olives.

62 And early in the morning he came again into the temple, and all the people came unto him; and he sat down, and taught them.

63 And the scribes and the Pharisees bring a woman taken in adultery; and having set her in the midst,

64 They say unto him, Master, this woman hath been taken in adultery in the very act.

65 Now in the law Moses commanded us to stone such: what then sayest thou of her?

66 And this t h e y said, tempting him t h a t they might have *whereof* to accuse him. But J e s u s stooped down, and with his finger wrote on the ground.

67 But when they continued asking him, he lifted up himself, and said unto them, He that is without sin among you, let him first cast a stone at her.

68 And again he stooped down, and with his finger wrote on the ground.

69 And they, when they heard it, went out one by one beginning from the eldest, *even* unto the last: and Jesus was left alone, and the woman, where she was, in the midst.

70 And J e s u s lifted up himself and said unto her, Woman, where are they? did no man condemn thee?

71 And she said, No man, Lord. And J e s u s s a i d, Neither do I condemn thee: go thy way; from henceforth sin no more.]

## CHAPTER XXXIV.

AGAIN therefore Jesus spake unto them, saying, I am the light of the world: he that followeth me shall not walk in the darkness, but shall have the light of life.

2 The Pharisees therefore said unto him, Thou bearest witness of thyself; thy witness is not true.

3 Jesus answered and said

"Neither do I Condemn Thee."

unto them, Even if I bear witness of myself, my witness is true; for I know whence I came, and whither I go; but ye know not whence I come, or whither I go.

4 Ye judge after the flesh; I judge no man.

5 Yea and if I judge, my judgement is true; for I am not alone, but I and the Father that sent me.

6 Yea and in your law it is written, that the witness of two men is true.

7 I am he that beareth witness of myself, and the Father that sent me beareth witness of me.

8 They said therefore unto him, Where is thy Father? Jesus answered, Ye know neither me, nor my Father: if ye knew me, ye would know my Father also.

9 These words spake he in the treasury, as he taught in the temple: and no man took him; because his hour was not yet come.

10 He said therefore again unto them, I go away, and ye shall seek me, and shall die in your sin: whither I go, ye cannot come.

11 The Jews therefore said, Will he kill himself, that he saith, Whither I go, ye cannot come?

12 And he said unto them, Ye are from beneath; I am from above: ye are of this world; I am not of this world.

13 I said therefore unto you, that ye shall die in your sins: for except ye believe that I am he, ye shall die in your sins.

14 They said therefore unto him, Who art thou? Jesus said unto them, Even that which I have also spoken unto you from the beginning.

15 I have many things to speak and to judge concerning you: howbeit he that sent me is true; and the things which I heard from him, these speak I unto the world.

16 They perceived not that he spake to them of the Father.

17 Jesus therefore said, When ye have lifted up the Son of man, then shall ye know that I am *he*, and *that* I do nothing of myself, but as the Father taught me, I speak these things.

18 And he that sent me is with me; he hath not left me alone; for I do always the things that are pleasing to him.

19 As he spake these things, many believed on him.

20 Jesus therefore said to those Jews which had believed him, If ye abide in my word, *then* are ye truly my disciples;

21 And ye shall know the truth, and the truth shall make you free. .

22 They answered unto him, We be Abraham's seed, and have never yet been in bondage to any man: how sayest thou, Ye shall be made free?

23 Jesus answered them, Verily, verily, I say unto you, Every one that com-mitteth sin is the bondservant of sin.

24 And the bondservant abideth not in the house for ever: the son abideth for ever.

25 If therefore the Son shall make you free, ye shall be free indeed.

26 I know that ye are Abraham's seed; yet ye seek to kill me, because my word hath not free course in you.

27 I speak the things which I have seen with *my* Father: and ye also do the things which ye heard from *your* father.

28 They answered and said unto him, Our father is Abraham. Jesus saith unto them, If ye were Abraham's children, ye would do the works of Abraham.

29 But now ye seek to kill me, a man that hath told you the truth, which I heard from God: this did not Abraham.

30 Ye do the works of your father. They said unto him, We were not born of forni-

THE TEMPLE BUILT BY HEROD.

cation; we have one Father, *even* God.

31 Jesus said unto them, If God were your Father, ye would love me: for I came forth and am come from God; for neither have I come of myself, but he sent me.

32 Why do ye not understand my speech? *Even* because ye cannot hear my word.

33 Ye are of *your* father the devil, and the lusts of your father it is your will to do. He was a murderer from the beginning, and stood not in the truth, because there is no truth in him. When he speaketh a lie, he speaketh of his own: for he is a liar, and the father thereof.

34 But because I say the truth, ye believe me not.

35 Which of you convicteth me of sin? If I say truth, why do ye not believe me?

36 He that is of God heareth the words of God: for this cause ye hear *them* not, because ye are not of God.

37 The Jews answered and said unto him, Say we not well that thou art a Samaritan, and hast a devil?

38 Jesus answered, I have not a devil; but I honour my Father, and ye dishonor me.

39 But I seek not mine own glory: there is one that seeketh and judgeth.

40 Verily, verily, I say unto you, If a man keep my word, he shall never see death.

41 The Jews said unto him, Now we know that thou hast a devil. Abraham is dead, and the prophets; and thou sayest, If a man keep my word, he shall never taste of death.

42 Art thou greater than our father Abraham, which is dead? and the prophets are dead: whom makest thou thyself?

43 Jesus answered, If I glorify myself, my glory is nothing: it is my Father that glorifieth me; of whom ye say, that he is your God;

44 And ye have not known

him: but I know him; and if I should say, I know him not, I shall be like unto you, a liar: but I know him, and keep his word.

45 Your father Abraham rejoiced to see my day; and he saw it, and was glad.

46 The Jews therefore said unto him, Thou art not yet fifty years old, and hast thou seen Abraham?

47 Jesus said unto them, Verily, verily, I say unto you, Before Abraham was, I am.

48 They took up stones therefore to cast at him: but Jesus hid himself, and went out of the temple.

## CHAPTER XXXV.

### THE BLIND MAN AND THE PHARISEES.

#### October, A. D. 29.

AND as Jesus passed by, he saw a man blind from his birth.

2 And his disciples asked him, saying, Rabbi, who did sin, this man, or his parents, that he should be born blind?

3 Jesus answered, Neither did this man sin nor his parents: but that the works of God should be made manifest in him.

4 We must work the works of him that sent me, while it is day: the night cometh, when no man can work.

5 When I am in the world I am the light of the world.

6 When he had thus spoken, he spat on the ground, and made clay of the spittle, and anointed his eyes with the clay,

7 And said unto him, Go, wash in the pool of Siloam (which is by interpretation, Sent). He went away therefore, and washed, and came seeing.

8 The neighbours therefore, and they which saw him aforetime, that he was a beggar, said, Is not this he that sat and begged?

9 Others said, It is he: others said, No, but he is like him. He said, I am he.

10 They said therefore unto him, How then were thine eyes opened?

JESUS HEALING THE BLIND BEGGAR.

11 He answered, The man that is called Jesus made clay, and anointed mine eyes, and said unto me, Go to Siloam, and wash: so I went away and washed, and I received sight.

12 And they said unto him, Where is he? He saith, I know not.

13 They bring to the Pharisees him that aforetime was blind.

14 Now it was the sabbath on the day when Jesus made the clay, and opened his eyes.

15 Again therefore t h e Pharisees also asked him how he received his sight. And he said unto them He put clay upon mine eyes, and I washed, and do see.

16 Some therefore of the Pharisees said, This man is not from God, because he keepeth not the sabbath. But others said, How can a man that is a sinner do such signs? And there was a division among them.

17 They say therefore un-

to the blind man again, What sayest thou of him, in that he opened thine eyes? And he said, He is a prophet.

18 The Jews therefore did not believe concerning him, that he had been blind, and had received his sight, until they called the parents of him that had received his sight,

19 And asked them, saying, Is this your son, who ye say was born blind? how then doth he now see?

20 His parents answered and said, We know that this is our son, and that he was born blind:

21 But how he now seeth, we know not; or who opened his eyes, we know not: ask him; he is of age; he shall speak for himself.

22 These things said his parents, because they feared the Jews: for the Jews had agreed already, that if any man should confess him *to be* Christ, he should be put out of the synagogue.

23 Therefore said his pa-

rents, He is of age; ask him.

24 So they called a second time the man that was blind, and said unto him, Give glory to God: we know that this man is a sinner.

25 He therefore answered, Whether he be a sinner, I know not: one thing I know, that, whereas I was blind, now I see.

26 They said therefore unto him, What did he to thee? how opened he thine eyes?

27 He answered them, I told you even now, and ye did not hear: wherefore would ye hear it again? would ye also become his disciples?

28 And they reviled him, and said, Thou art his disciple; but we are disciples of Moses.

29 We know that God hath spoken unto Moses: but as for this man, we know not whence he is.

30 The man answered and said unto them, Why, herein is the marvel, that ye know not whence he is, and *yet* he opened mine eyes.

31 We know that God heareth not sinners: but if any man be a worshipper of God, and do his will, him he heareth.

32 Since the world began it was never heard that any one opened the eyes of a man born blind.

33 If this man were not from God, he could do nothing.

34 They answered and said unto him, Thou wast altogether born in sins, and dost thou teach us? And they cast him out.

35 Jesus heard that they had cast him out; and finding him, he said, Dost thou believe on the Son of God?

36 He answered and said, And who is he, Lord, that I may believe on him?

37 Jesus said unto him, Thou hast both seen him, and he it is that speaketh with thee.

38 And he said, Lord, I

"Dost Thou Believe on the Son of God?"

believe. And he worshipped him.

39 And Jesus said, For judgement came I into this world, that they which see not may see; and that they which see may become blind.

40 Those of the Pharisees which were with him heard these things, and said unto him, Are we also blind?

41 Jesus said unto them, If ye were blind, ye would have no sin: but now ye say, We see: your sin remaineth.

## CHAPTER XXXVI.
### October, A. D. 29.

VERILY, verily, I say unto you, He that entereth not by the door into the fold of the sheep, but climbeth up some other way, the same is a thief and a robber.

2 But he that entereth in by the door is the shepherd of the sheep.

3 To him the porter openeth; and the sheep hear his voice: and he calleth his own sheep by name, and leadeth them out.

4 When he hath put forth all his own, he goeth before them, and the sheep follow him: for they know his voice.

5 And a stranger will they not follow, but will flee from him: for they know not the voice of strangers.

6 This parable spake Jesus unto them; but they understood not what things they were which he spake unto them.

7 Jesus therefore said unto them again, Verily, verily I say unto you, I am the door of the sheep.

8 All that came before me are thieves and robbers: but the sheep did not hear them.

9 I am the door: by me if any man enter in, he shall be saved, and shall go in and go out, and shall find pasture.

10 The thief cometh not, but that he may steal, and kill, and destroy: I came that they may have life, and may have it abundantly.

11 I am the good shepherd: the good shepherd

layeth down his life for the sheep.

12 He that is a hireling, and not a shepherd, whose own the sheep are not, beholdeth the wolf coming, and leaveth the sheep and fleeth, and the wolf snatcheth them, and scattereth *them:*

13 *He fleeth* because he is a hireling, and careth not for the sheep.

14 I am the good shepherd; and I know mine own, and mine own know me,

15 Even as the Father knoweth me, and I know the Father; and I lay down my life for the sheep.

16 And other sheep I have, which are not of this fold: them also I must bring, and they shall hear my voice; and they shall become one flock, one shepherd.

17 Therefore doth the Father love me, because I lay down my life, that I may take it again.

18 No one taketh it away from me, but I lay it down of myself. I have power to lay it down, and I have power to take it again. This commandment received I from my Father.

19 There arose a division again among the Jews because of these words.

20 And many of them said, He hath a devil, and is mad; why hear ye him?

21 Others said, These are not the sayings of one possessed with a devil. Can a devil open the eyes of the blind?

22 And it was the feast of the dedication at Jerusalem: it was winter;

23 And Jesus was walking in the temple in Solomon's porch.

24 The Jews therefore came round about him, and said unto him, How long dost thou hold us in suspense? If thou art the Christ, tell us plainly.

25 Jesus answered them, I told you, and ye believe not: the works that I do in my Father's name, these bear witness of me.

" The Good Shepherd."

26 But ye believe not, because ye are not of my sheep.

27 My sheep hear my voice, and I know them, and they follow me:

28 And I give unto them eternal life, and they shall never perish, and no one shall snatch them out of my hand.

29 My Father, which hath given *them* unto me, is greater than all; and no one is able to snatch *them* out of the Father's hand.

30 I and the Father are one.

31 The Jews took up stones again to stone him.

32 Jesus answered them, Many good works have I shewed you from the Father; for which of those works do ye stone me?

33 The Jews answered him, For a good work we stone thee not, but for blasphemy; and because that thou, being a man, makest thyself God.

34 Jesus answered them, Is it not written in your law, I said, Ye are gods?

35 If he called them gods, unto whom the word of God came (and the scripture cannot be broken),

36 Say ye of him, whom the Father sanctified and sent into the world, Thou blasphemest; because I said I am *the* Son of God?

37 If I do not the works of my Father, believe me not.

38 But if I do them, though ye believe not me, believe the works: that ye may know and understand that the Father is in me, and I in the Father.

39 They sought again to take him: and he went forth out of their hand.

40 And he went away again beyond Jordan into the place where John was at the first baptizing; and there he abode.

41 And many came unto him; and they said, John indeed did no sign: but all things whatsoever John spake of this man were true.

42 And many believed on him there.

## CHAPTER XXXVII.

### THE LAW OF DIVORCE.

AND there came unto him Pharisees, and asked him, Is it lawful for a man to put away *his* wife? tempting him.

2 And he answered and said unto them, What did Moses command you?

3 And they said, Moses suffered to write a bill of divorcement, and to put her away.

4 But Jesus said unto them, For your hardness of heart he wrote you this commandment.

5 But from the beginning of creation, Male and female made he them.

6 For this cause shall a man leave his father and mother, and shall cleave to his wife;

7 And the twain shall become one flesh: so that they are no more twain, but one flesh.

8 What therefore God hath joined together, let not man put asunder.

9 And in the house the disciples asked him again of this matter.

10 And he saith unto them, Whosoever shall put away his wife, and marry another, committeth adultery against her:

11 And if she herself shall put away her husband and marry another, she committeth adultery.

12 The disciples say unto him, if the case of the man is so with his wife, it is not expedient to marry.

13 But he said unto them, All men cannot receive this saying, but they to whom it is given.

14 For there are eunuchs, which were so born from their mother's womb: and there are eunuchs, which were made eunuchs by men: and there are eunuchs, which made themselves eunuchs for the kingdom of heaven's sake.

15 He that is able to receive it, let him receive it.

"Suffer the Little Children to Come unto Me."

### LITTLE CHILDREN.

16 And they brought unto him little children, that he should touch them: and the disciples rebuked them.

17 But when Jesus saw it, he was moved with indignation, and said unto them, Suffer the little children to come unto me; forbid them not: for of such is the kingdom of God.

18 Verily I say unto you, Whosoever shall not receive the kingdom of God as a little child, he shall in no wise enter therein.

19 And he took them in his arms, and blessed them, laying his hands upon them.

20 And as he was going forth into the way, there ran one to him, and kneeled to him, and asked him, Good Master, what shall I do that I may inherit eternal life?

21 And Jesus said unto him, Why callest thou me good? none is good save one, *even* God.

22 But if thou wouldest enter into life, keep the commandments.

23 He saith unto him, Which? And Jesus said, Thou shalt not kill, Thou shalt not commit adultery, Thou shalt not steal, Thou shalt not bear false witness,

24 Honour thy father and thy mother: and, Thou shalt love thy neighbour as thyself.

25 The young man saith unto him, All these things have I observed: what lack I yet?

26 And Jesus looking upon him loved him, and said unto him, One thing thou lackest: If thou wouldest be perfect, go, sell that thou hast, and give to the poor, and thou shalt have treasure in heaven: and come, follow me.

27 But when the young man heard the saying, he went away sorrowful: for he was one that had great possessions.

28 And Jesus looked round about, and saith unto his disciples, How hardly shall

they that have riches enter into the kingdom of God!

29 And the disciples were amazed at his words. But Jesus answereth again, and saith unto them, Children, how hard is it for them that trust in riches to enter into the kingdom of God!

30 It is easier for a camel to go through a needle's eye, than for a rich man to enter into the kingdom of God.

31 And they were astonished exceedingly, saying unto him, Then who can be saved?

32 Jesus looking upon them saith, With men it is impossible, but not with God: for all things are possible with God.

33 Then answered Peter and said unto him, Lo, we have left all, and followed thee; what then shall we have?

34 And Jesus said unto them, Verily I say unto you, that ye which have followed me, in the regeneration when the Son of man shall sit on the throne of his glory, ye also shall sit upon twelve thrones, judging the twelve tribes of Israel.

35 And every one that hath left houses, or brethren, or sisters, or father, or mother, or children, or lands, for my name's sake, shall receive a hundredfold, and shall inherit eternal life.

36 But many shall be last *that are* first; and first *that are* last.

37 For the kingdom of heaven is like unto a man that is a householder, which went out early in the morning to hire labourers into his vineyard.

38 And when he had agreed with the labourers for a penny a day, he sent them into his vineyard.

39 And he went out about the third hour, and saw others standing in the marketplace idle.

40 And to them he said, Go ye also into the vineyard, and whatsoever is right I

will give you. And they went their way.

41 Again he went out about the sixth and the ninth hour, and did likewise.

42 And about the eleventh *hour* he went out, and found others standing; and he saith unto them, Why stand ye here all the day idle?

43 They say unto him, Because no man hath hired us. He saith unto them, Go ye also into the vineyard.

44 And when even was come, the lord of the vineyard saith unto his steward, Call the labourers, and pay them their hire, beginning from the last unto the first.

45 And when they came that *were hired* about the eleventh hour, they received every man a penny.

46 And when the first came, they supposed that they would receive more; and they likewise received every man a penny.

47 And when they received it, they murmured against the householder, saying,

48 These last have spent *but* one hour, and thou hast made them equal unto us, which have borne the burden of the day and the scorching heat.

49 But he answered and said to one of them, Friend, I do thee no wrong: didst not thou agree with me for a penny?

50 Take up that which is thine, and go thy way; it is my will to give unto this last, even as unto thee.

51 Is it not lawful for me to do what I will with mine own?

52 Or is thine eye evil, because I am good? So the last shall be first and the first last.

## CHAPTER XXXVIII.

### THE SABBATH AND GOOD WORKS.

AND he was teaching in one of the synagogues on the sabbath day.

2 And behold, a woman which had a spirit of infirmity eighteen years; and she

was bowed together, and could in no wise lift herself up.

3 And when Jesus saw her he called her, and said to her, Woman, thou art loosed from thine infirmity.

4 And he laid his hands upon her: and immediately she was made straight, and glorified God.

5 And the ruler of the synagogue, being moved with indignation because Jesus had healed on the sabbath, answered and said to the multitude, There are six days in which men ought to work: in them therefore come and be healed, and not on the day of the sabbath.

6 But the Lord answered him, and said, Ye hypocrites, doth not each one of you on the sabbath loose his ox or his ass from the stall, and lead him away to watering?

7 And ought not this woman, being a daughter of Abraham, whom Satan had bound, lo, *these* eighteen years, to have been loosed from this bond on the day of the sabbath?

8 And as he said these things, all his adversaries were put to shame: and all the multitude rejoiced for all the glorious things that were done by him.

9 He said therefore, Unto what is the kingdom of God like? and whereunto shall I liken it?

10 It is like unto a grain of mustard seed, which a man took, and cast into his own garden; and it grew, and became a tree; and the birds of the heaven lodged in the branches thereof.

11 And again he said, Whereunto shall I liken the kingdom of God?

12 It is like unto leaven, which a woman took and hid in three measures of meal, till it was all leavened.

13 And one said unto him, Lord, are they few that be saved? And he said unto them,

14 Strive to enter in by the narrow door: for many,

"Woman, Thou art Loosed from Thine Infirmity."

I say unto you, shall seek to enter in, and shall not be able.

15 When once the master of the house is risen up, and hath shut to the door, and ye begin to stand without, and to knock at the door, saying, Lord, open to us; and he shall answer and say to you, I know you not whence ye are:

16 Then shall ye begin to say, We did eat and drink in thy presence, and thou didst teach in our streets:

17 And he shall say, I tell you, I know not whence ye are; depart from me, all ye workers of iniquity.

18 There shall be the weeping and gnashing of teeth, when ye shall see Abraham, and Isaac, and Jacob, and all the prophets, in the kingdom of God, and yourselves cast forth without.

19 And they shall come from the east and west, and from the north and south, and shall sit down in the kingdom of God.

20 And behold, there are last which shall be first, and there are first which shall be last.

21 In that very hour there came certain Pharisees, saying to him, Get thee out, and go hence: for Herod would fain kill thee.

22 And he said unto them, Go and say to that fox, Behold, I cast out devils and perform cures to-day and to-morrow, and the third *day* I am perfected.

23 Howbeit I must go on my way to-day and to-morrow and the *day* following: for it cannot be that a prophet perish out of Jerusalem.

24 O Jerusalem, Jerusalem, which killeth the prophets, and stoneth them that are sent unto her! how often would I have gathered thy children together, even as a hen *gathereth* her own brood under her wings, and ye would not!

25 Behold your house is left unto you *desolate*: and I say unto you, Ye shall not

see me, until ye shall say, Blessed *is* he that cometh in the name of the Lord.

### THE SABBATH AND THE PHARISEES.

26 And it came to pass, when he went into the house of one of the rulers of the Pharisees on a sabbath to eat bread, that they were watching him.

27 And behold, there was before him a certain man which had the dropsy.

28 And Jesus answering spake unto the lawyers and Pharisees, saying, Is it lawful to heal on the sabbath, or not?

29 But they held their peace. And he took him, and healed him, and let him go.

30 And he said unto them, Which of you shall have an ass or an ox fallen into a well, and will not straightway draw him up on a sabbath day?

31 And they could not answer again unto these things.

### THE CHIEF SEATS.

32 And he spake a parable unto those which were bidden, when he marked how they chose out the chief seats; saying unto them,

33 When thou art bidden of any man to a marriage feast, sit not down in the chief seat; lest haply a more honourable man than thou be bidden of him,

34 And he that bade thee and him shall come and say to thee, Give this man place; and then thou shalt begin with shame to take the lowest place.

35 But when thou art bidden, go and sit down in the lowest place; that when he that hath bidden thee cometh he may say to thee, Friend, go up higher: then shalt thou have glory in the presence of all that sit at meat with thee.

36 For every one that exalteth himself shall be humbled; and he that humbleth himself shall be exalted.

37 And he said to him also

"Is it Lawful to Heal on the Sabbath or Not?"

that had bidden him, When thou makest a dinner or a supper, call not thy friends, nor thy brethren, nor thy kinsmen, nor rich neighbours; lest haply they also bid thee again, and a recompense be made thee.

38 But when thou makest a feast, bid the poor, the maimed, the lame, the blind:

39 And thou shalt be blessed; because they have not *wherewith* to recompense thee: for thou shalt be recompensed in the resurrection of the just.

40 And when one of them that sat at meat with him heard these things, he said unto him, Blessed is he that shall eat bread in the kingdom of God.

41 But he said unto him, A certain man made a great supper; and he bade many:

42 And he sent forth his servant at supper time to say to them that were bidden, Come; for *all* things are now ready.

43 And they all with one

*consent* began to make excuse. The first said unto him, I have bought a field, and I must needs go out and see it: I pray thee have me excused.

44 And another said, I have bought five yoke of oxen, and I go to prove them: I pray thee have me excused.

45 And another said, I have married a wife, and therefore I cannot come.

46 And the servant came, and told his lord these things. Then the master of the house being angry said to his servant, Go out quickly into the streets and lanes of the city, and bring in hither the poor and maimed and blind and lame.

47 And the servant said, Lord, what thou didst command is done, and yet there is room.

48 And the lord said unto the servant, Go out into the highways and hedges, and constrain *them* to come in, that my house may be filled.

49 For I say unto you,

that none of those men which were bidden shall taste of my supper.

## CHAPTER XXXIX.

### THE CROSS TO BE BORNE.

NOW there went with him great multitudes: and he turned, and said unto them,

2 If any man cometh unto me, and hateth not his own father, and mother, and wife, and children, and brethren, and sisters, yea, and his own life also, he cannot be my disciple.

3 Whosoever doth not bear his own cross, and come after me, cannot be my disciple.

4 For which of you, desiring to build a tower, doth not first sit down and count the cost, whether he have *wherewith* to complete it?

5 Lest haply, when he hath laid a foundation, and is not able to finish, all that behold begin to mock him, saying,

6 This man began to build, and was not able to finish.

7 Or what king, as he goeth to encounter another king in war, will not sit down first and take counsel whether he is able with ten thousand to meet him that cometh against him with twenty thousand?

8 Or else, while the other is yet a great way off, he sendeth an ambassage, and asketh conditions of peace.

9 So therefore whosoever he be of you that renounceth not all that he hath, he cannot be my disciple.

10 Salt therefore is good: but if even the salt have lost its savour, wherewith shall it be seasoned?

11 It is fit neither for the land nor for the dunghill: *men* cast it out. He that hath ears to hear, let him hear.

12 Now all the publicans and sinners were drawing near unto him for to hear him.

13 And both the Pharisees and the scribes murmured, saying, This man receiveth sinners, and eateth with them.

"COME, FOR ALL THINGS ARE NOW READY."

### THE LOST SHEEP.

December, A. D. 29.

14 And he spake unto them this parable, saying,

15 What man of you, having a hundred sheep, and having lost one of them, doth not leave the ninety and nine in the wilderness, and go after that which is lost until he find it?

16 And when he hath found it, he layeth it on his shoulders, rejoicing.

17 And when he cometh home, he calleth together his friends and his neighbours, saying unto them, Rejoice with me, for I have found my sheep which was lost.

18 I say unto you, that even so there shall be joy in heaven over one sinner that repenteth, *more* than over ninety and nine righteous persons, which need no repentance.

19 Or what woman having ten pieces of silver, if she lose one piece, doth not light a lamp, and sweep the house, and seek diligently until she find it?

20 And when she hath found it, she calleth together her friends and neighbours, saying, Rejoice with me, for I have found the piece which I had lost.

21 Even so, I say unto you, there is joy in the presence of the angels of God over one sinner that repenteth.

### THE PRODIGAL SON.

22 And he said, A certain man had two sons:

23 And the younger of them said to his father, Father, give me the portion of *thy* substance that falleth to me. And he divided unto them his living.

24 And not many days after the younger son gathered all together, and took his journey into a far country; and there he wasted his substance with riotous living.

25 And when he had spent all, 'there arose a mighty famine in that country; and he began to be in want.

26 And he went and joined himself to one of the citizens of that country; and he sent him into his fields to feed swine.

27 And he would fain have been filled with the husks that the swine did eat: and no man gave unto him.

28 But when he came to himself he said, How many hired servants of my father's have bread enough and to spare, and I perish here with hunger!

29 I will arise and go to my father, and will say unto him, Father, I have sinned against heaven, and in thy sight:

30 I am no more worthy to be called thy son: make me as one of thy hired servants.

31 And he arose, and came to his father. But while he was yet afar off, his father saw him, and was moved with compassion, and ran, and fell on his neck, and kissed him.

32 And the son said unto him, Father, I have sinned against heaven, and in thy sight: I am no more worthy to be called thy son.

33 But the father said to his servants, Bring forth quickly the best robe, and put it on him; and put a ring on his hand, and shoes on his feet:

34 And bring the fatted calf, *and* kill it, and let us eat, and make merry:

35 For this my son was dead, and is alive again; he was lost, and is found. And they began to be merry.

36 Now his elder son was in the field: and as he came and drew nigh to the house, he heard music and dancing.

37 And he called to him one of the servants, and inquired what these things might be.

38 And he said unto him, Thy brother is come; and thy father hath killed the fatted calf, because he hath received him safe and sound.

39 But he was angry, and would not go in: and his

father came out, and en-
treated him.

40 But he answered and
said to his father, Lo, these
many years do I serve thee,
and I never transgressed a
commandment of thine: and
*yet* thou never gavest me a
kid, that I might make merry
with my friends:

41 But when this thy son
came, which hath devoured
thy living with harlots, thou
killedst for him the fatted
calf.

42 And he said unto him,
Son, thou art ever with me,
and all that is mine is thine.

43 But it was meet to make
merry and be glad: for this
thy brother was dead, and is
alive *again*; and *was* lost,
and is found.

## CHAPTER XL.

### THE UNJUST STEWARD.

AND he said also unto
the disciples, There was
a certain rich man, which
had a steward; and the same
was accused unto him that
he was wasting his goods.

2 And he called him, and
said unto him, What is this
that I hear of thee? render
the account of thy stewardship; for thou canst be no
longer steward.

3 And the steward said
within himself, What shall I
do, seeing that my lord
taketh away the stewardship
from me? I have not strength
to dig; to beg I am ashamed.

4 I am resolved what to
do, that, when I am put out
of the stewardship, they
may receive me into their
houses.

5 And calling to him each
one of his lord's debtors, he
said to the first, How much
owest thou unto my lord?

6 And he said, A hundred
measures of oil. And he
said unto him, Take thy
bond, and sit down quickly
and write fifty.

7 Then said he to another
And how much owest thou?
And he said, A hundred
measures of wheat. He
saith unto him, Take thy
bond, and write fourscore.

8 And his lord commended the unrighteous steward because he had done wisely: for the sons of this world are for their own generation wiser than the sons of the light.

9 And I say unto you, Make to yourselves friends by means of the mammon of unrighteousness; that, when it shall fail, they may receive you into the eternal tabernacles.

10 He that is faithful in a very little is faithful also in much: and he that is unrighteous in a very little is unrighteous also in much.

11 If therefore ye have not been faithful in the unrighteous mammon, who will commit to your trust the true *riches?*

12 And if ye have not been faithful in that which is another's, who will give you that which is your own?

13 No servant can serve two masters: for either he will hate the one, and love the other; or else he will hold to one, and despise the other. Ye cannot serve God and mammon.

14 And the Pharisees, who were lovers of money, heard all these things; and they scoffed at him.

15 And he said unto them, Ye are they that justify yourselves in the sight of men; but God knoweth your hearts: for that which is exalted among men is an abomination in the sight of God.

16 The law and the prophets *were* until John: from that time the gospel of the kingdom of God is preached, and every man entereth violently into it.

17 But it is easier for heaven and earth to pass away, than for one tittle of the law to fall.

18 Every one that putteth away his wife, and marrieth another, committeth adultery: and he that marrieth one that is put away from a husband committeth adultery.

THE RICH MAN FARING SUMPTUOUSLY.

THE RICH MAN AND
LAZARUS.

November, A. D. 29.

19 Now there was a certain rich man, and he was clothed in purple and fine linen, faring sumptuously every day:

20 And a certain beggar named Lazarus was laid at his gate, full of sores,

21 And desiring to be fed with the *crumbs* that fell from the rich man's table; yea, even the dogs came and licked his sores.

22 And it came to pass, that the beggar died, and that he was carried away by the angels into Abraham's bosom: and the rich man also died, and was buried.

23 And in Hades he lifted up his eyes, being in torments, and seeth Abraham afar off, and Lazarus in his bosom.

24 And he cried and said, Father Abraham, have mercy on me, and send Lazarus, that he may dip the tip of his finger in water, and cool my tongue; for I am in anguish in this flame.

25 But Abraham said, Son, remember that thou in thy lifetime receivedst thy good things, and Lazarus in like manner evil things: but now here he is comforted, and thou art in anguish.

26 And beside all this, between us and you there is a great gulf fixed, that they which would pass from hence to you may not be able, and that none may cross over from thence to us.

27 And he said, I pray thee therefore, father, that thou wouldest send him to my father's house;

28 For I have five brethren; that he may testify unto them, lest they also come into this place of torment.

29 But Abraham saith, They have Moses and the prophets; let them hear them.

30 And he said, Nay, father Abraham: but if one go to them from the dead they will repent.

31 And he said unto him, If they hear not Moses and the prophets, neither will they be persuaded, if one rise from the dead.

32 And he said unto his disciples, It is impossible but that occasions of stumbling should come: but woe unto him, through whom they come!

33 It were well for him if a millstone were hanged about his neck, and he were thrown into the sea, rather than that he should cause one of these little ones to stumble.

34 Take heed to yourselves: if thy brother sin, rebuke him; and if he repent, forgive him.

35 And if he sin against thee seven times in the day, and seven times turn again to thee, saying, I repent; thou shalt forgive him.

36 And the apostles said unto the Lord, Increase our faith.

37 And the Lord said, If ye have faith as a grain of mustard seed, ye would say unto this sycamine tree, Be thou rooted up, and be thou planted in the sea; and it would have obeyed you.

38 But who is there of you having a servant plowing or keeping sheep, that will say unto him, when he is come in from the field, Come straightway and sit down to meat;

39 And will not rather say unto him, Make ready wherewith I may sup, and gird thyself, and serve me, till I have eaten and drunken; and afterward thou shalt eat and drink?

40 Doth he thank the servant because he did the things that were commanded?

41 Even so ye also, when ye shall have done all the things that are commanded you, say, We are unprofitable servants; we have done that which it was our duty to do.

"BETWEEN US AND YOU THERE IS A GREAT GULF FIXED."

## CHAPTER XLI.
### THE KINGDOM OF GOD WITHIN.

AND being asked by the Pharisees, when the kingdom of God cometh, he answered them and said, The kingdom of God cometh not with observation:

2 Neither shall they say, Lo, here! or, There! for lo, the kingdom of God is within you.

3 And he said unto the disciples, T h e days will come, when ye shall desire to see one of the days of the Son of man, and ye shall not see it.

4 And they shall say to you, Lo, there! Lo, here! go not away, nor follow after *them*.

5 For as the lightning, when it lighteneth out of the one part under the heaven, shineth unto the other part under heaven; so shall the Son of man be in his day.

6 But first must he suffer many things and be rejected of this generation.

7 And as it came to pass in the days of Noah, even so shall it be also in the days of the Son of man.

8 They ate, they drank, and they married, they were given in marriage, until the day that Noah entered into the ark, and the flood came, and destroyed them all.

9 Likewise even as it came to pass in the days of Lot; they ate, they drank, they bought, they sold, they planted, they builded;

10 But in the day that Lot went out from Sodom it rained fire and brimstone from heaven, and destroyed them all:

11 After the same manner shall it be in the day that the Son of man is revealed.

12 In that day, he which shall be on the housetop, and his goods in the house, let him not go down to take them away: and let him that is in the field likewise not return back.

13 Remember Lot's wife. Whosoever shall seek to gain

his life shall lose it: but whosoever shall lose *his life* shall preserve it.

14 I say unto you, In that night there shall be two men on one bed; the one shall be taken, and the other shall be left.

15 There shall be two women grinding together; the one shall be taken, and the other shall be left.

16 And they answering say unto him, Where, Lord? And he said unto them, Where the body *is*, thither will the eagles also be gathered together.

### THE UNJUST JUDGE.

17 And he spake a parable unto them to the end that they ought always to pray, and not to faint;

18 Saying, There was in a city a judge, which feared not God, and regarded not man:

19 And there was a widow in that city; and she came oft unto him, saying, Avenge me of mine adversary.

20 And he would not for a while: but afterward he said within himself, Though I fear not God, nor regard man;

21 Yet because this widow troubleth me, I will avenge her, lest she wear me out by her continual coming.

22 And the Lord said, Hear what the unrighteous judge saith.

23 And shall not God avenge his elect, which cry to him day and night, and he is longsuffering over them?

24 I say unto you, that he will avenge them speedily. Howbeit when the Son of man cometh, shall he find faith on the earth?

### SELF-RIGHTEOUSNESS.

25 And he spake also this parable unto certain which trusted in themselves that they were righteous, and set all others at naught:

26 Two men went up into the temple to pray; the one a Pharisee, and the other a publican.

27 The Pharisee stood and prayed thus with himself,

THE PHARISEE AND THE PUBLICAN

God, I thank thee, that I am not as the rest of men, extortioners, unjust, adulterers, or even as this publican.

28 I fast twice in the week; I give tithes of all that I get.

29 But the publican, standing afar off, would not lift up so much as his eyes unto heaven, but smote his breast, saying, God, be merciful to me a sinner.

30 I say unto you, This man went down to his house justified rather than the other: for every one that exalteth himself shall be humbled; but he that humbleth himself shall be exalted.

## CHAPTER XLII.

### LAZARUS.

NOW a certain man was sick, Lazarus of Bethany, of the village of Mary and her sister Martha.

2 And it was that Mary which anointed the Lord with ointment, and wiped his feet with her hair, whose brother Lazarus was sick.

3 The sisters therefore sent unto him, saying, Lord, behold, he whom thou lovest is sick.

4 But when Jesus heard it, he said, This sickness is not unto death, but for the glory of God, that the Son of God may be glorified thereby.

5 Now Jesus loved Martha, and her sister, and Lazarus.

6 When therefore he heard that he was sick, he abode at that time two days in the place where he was.

7 Then after this he saith to the disciples, Let us go into Judæa again.

8 The disciples say unto him, Rabbi, the Jews were but now seeking to stone thee; and goest thou thither again?

9 Jesus answered, Are there not twelve hours in the day? If a man walk in the day, he stumbleth not, because he seeth the light of this world.

10 But if a man walk in the night, he stumbleth, because the light is not in him.

11 These things spake he: and after this he saith unto them, Our friend Lazarus is fallen asleep; but I go, that I may awake him out of sleep.

12 The disciples therefore said unto him, Lord, if he is fallen asleep, he will recover.

13 Now Jesus had spoken of his death: but they thought that he spake of taking rest in sleep.

14 Then Jesus therefore said unto them plainly, Lazarus is dead.

15 And I am glad for your sakes that I was not there, to the intent ye may believe; nevertheless let us go unto him.

16 Thomas therefore, who is called Didymus, said unto his fellow-disciples, Let us also go, that we may die with him.

17 So when Jesus came, he found that he had been in the tomb four days already.

18 Now Bethany was nigh unto Jerusalem, about fifteen furlongs off;

19 And many of the Jews had come to Martha and Mary, to console them concerning their brother.

20 Martha therefore, when she heard that Jesus was coming, went and met him: but Mary still sat in the house.

21 Martha therefore said unto Jesus, Lord, if thou hadst been here, my brother had not died.

22 And even now I know that, whatsoever thou shalt ask of God, God will give thee. Jesus saith unto her,

23 Thy brother shall rise again.

24 Martha saith unto him, I know that he shall rise again in the resurrection at the last day.

25 Jesus said unto her, I am the resurrection, and the life: he that believeth on me, though he die, yet shall he live:

26 And whosoever liveth and believeth on me shall never die. Believest thou this?

LAZARUS SICK AT BETHANY.

27 She saith unto him, Yea, Lord: I have believed that thou art the Christ, the Son of God, *even* he that cometh into the world.

28 And when she had said this, she went away, and called Mary her sister secretly, saying, The Master is here, and calleth thee.

29 And she, when she heard it, arose quickly, and went unto him.

30 (Now Jesus was not yet come into the village, but was still in the place where Martha met him.)

31 The Jews then which were with her in the house, and were comforting her, when they saw Mary, that she rose up quickly and went out, followed her, supposing that she was going unto the tomb to weep there.

32 Mary therefore, when she came where Jesus was, and saw him, fell down at his feet, saying unto him, Lord, if thou hadst been here, my brother had not died.

33 When Jesus therefore saw her weeping, and the Jews *also* weeping which came with her, he groaned in the spirit, and was troubled, and said,

34 Where have ye laid him? They say unto him, Lord, come and see.

35 Jesus wept.

36 The Jews therefore said, Behold how he loved him!

37 But some of them said, Could not this man, which opened the eyes of him that was blind, have caused that this man also should not die?

38 Jesus therefore again groaning in himself cometh to the tomb. Now it was a cave, and a stone lay against it.

39 Jesus saith, Take ye away the stone. Martha, the sister of him that was dead, saith, unto him, Lord, by this time he stinketh: for he hath been *dead* four days.

40 Jesus saith unto her, Said I not unto thee, that, if thou believedst, thou

shouldest see the glory of God?

41 So they took away the stone. And Jesus lifted up his eyes. and said, Father. I thank thee that thou heardest me.

42 And I knew that thou hearest me always: but because of the multitude which standeth around I said it, that they may believe that thou didst send me.

January or February, A. D. 30.

43 And when he had thus spoken, he cried with a loud voice. Lazarus. come forth.

44 He that was dead came forth, bound hand and foot with grave-clothes; and his face was bound about with a napkin. Jesus saith unto them, Loose him, and let him go.

45 Many therefore of the Jews. which came to Mary and beheld that which he did. believed on him.

46 But some of them went away to the Pharisees. and told them the things which Jesus had done.

47 The chief priests therefore and the Pharisees gathered a council. and said, What do we? for this man doeth many signs.

48 If we let him thus alone. all men will believe on him: and the Romans will come and take away both our place and our nation.

49 But a certain one of them. Caiaphas, being high priest that year, said unto them, Ye know nothing at all.

50 Nor do ye take account that it is expedient for you that one man should die for the people. and that the whole nation perish not.

51 Now this he said not of himself. but being high priest that year, he prophesied that Jesus should die for the nation:

52 And not for the nation only, but that he might also gather together into one the children of God that are scattered abroad.

53 So from that day forth they took counsel that they might put him to death.

54 Jesus therefore walked no more openly among the Jews, but departed thence into the country near to the wilderness, into a city called Ephraim; and there he tarried with the disciples.

## CHAPTER XLIII.

### JESUS PREDICTS HIS DEATH.

AND they were in the way, going up to Jerusalem; and Jesus was going before them: and they were amazed; and they that followed were afraid.

2 And he took again the twelve, and began to tell them the things that were to happen unto him, *saying*,

3 Behold, we go up to Jerusalem; and the Son of man shall be delivered unto the chief priests and the scribes; and they shall condemn him to death, and shall deliver him unto the Gentiles:

4 And they shall mock him, and shall spit upon him, and shall scourge him, and shall kill him; and after three days he shall rise again.

5 And they understood none of these things; and this saying was hid from them, and they perceived not the things that were said.

### THE SONS OF ZEBEDEE.

6 Then came to him the mother of the sons of Zebedee with her sons, worshipping *him*, and asking a certain thing of him.

7 And he said unto her, What wouldest thou? She saith unto him, Command that these my two sons may sit, one on thy right hand, and one on thy left hand, in thy kingdom.

8 But Jesus answered and said, Ye know not what ye ask. Are ye able to drink the cup that I am about to drink? They say unto him, We are able.

9 He saith unto them, My cup indeed ye shall drink: but to sit on my right hand, and on *my* left hand, is not mine to give, but *it is for*

*them* for whom it hath been prepared of my Father.

10 And when the ten heard it, they were moved with indignation concerning the two brethren.

11 But Jesus called them unto him, and said, Ye know that the rulers of the Gentiles lord it over them, and their great ones exercise authority over them.

12 Not so shall it be among you: but whosoever would become great among you shall be your minister; and whosoever would be first among you shall be your servant:

13 Even as the Son of man came not to be ministered unto, but to minister, and to give his life a ransom for many.

### THE BLIND BARTIMÆUS.
#### March, A. D. 30.

14 And they come to Jericho: and as he went out from Jericho, with his disciples and a great multitude, the son of Timæus, Bartimæus, a blind beggar, was sitting by the way side.

15 And when he heard that it was Jesus of Nazareth, he began to cry out, and say, Jesus, thou son of David, have mercy on me.

16 And many rebuked him, that he should hold his peace: but he cried out the more a great deal, Thou son of David, have mercy on me.

17 And Jesus stood still, and said, Call ye him. And they call the blind man, saying unto him, Be of good cheer: rise, he calleth thee.

18 And he, casting away his garment, sprang up, and came to Jesus.

19 And Jesus answered him, and said, What wilt thou that I should do unto thee? And the blind man said unto him, Rabboni, that I may receive my sight.

20 And Jesus said unto him, Receive thy sight: thy faith hath made thee whole.

21 And immediately he received his sight, and followed him, glorifying God:

and all the people, when they saw it, gave praise unto God.

## ZACCHÆUS.

22 And he entered and was passing through Jericho. And behold, a man called by name Zacchæus; and he was a chief publican, and he was rich.

23 And he sought to see Jesus who he was; and could not for the crowd, because he was little of stature.

24 And he ran on before, and climbed up into a sycomore tree to see him: for he was to pass that way.

25 And when Jesus came to the place, he looked up, and said unto him, Zacchæus, make haste, and come down; for to-day I must abide at thy house.

26 And he made haste, and came down, and received him joyfully.

27 And when they saw it, they all murmured, saying, He is gone in to lodge with a man that is a sinner.

28 And Zacchæus stood, and said unto the Lord, Behold, Lord, the half of my goods I give to the poor; and if I have wrongfully exacted aught of any man, I restore fourfold.

29 And Jesus said unto him, To-day is salvation come to this house, forasmuch as he also is a son of Abraham.

30 For the Son of man came to seek and to save that which was lost.

## THE MISUSED TALENT.

31 And as they heard these things, he added and spake a parable, because he was nigh to Jerusalem, and *because* they supposed that the kingdom of God was immediately to appear.

32 He said therefore, A certain nobleman went into a far country, to receive for himself a kingdom, and to return.

33 And he called ten servants of his, and gave them ten pounds, and said unto them Trade ye *herewith* till I come.

34 But his citizens hated him, and sent an ambassage after him, saying, We will not that this man reign over us.

35 And it came to pass, when he was come back again, having received the kingdom, that he commanded these servants, unto whom he had given the money, to be called to him, that he might know what they had gained by trading.

36 And the first came before him, saying, Lord, thy pound hath made ten pounds more.

37 And he said unto him, Well done, thou good servant: because thou wast found faithful in a very little, have thou authority over ten cities.

38 And the second came, saying, Thy pound, Lord, hath made five pounds.

39 And he said unto him also, Be thou also over five cities.

40 And another came saying, Lord, behold, *here is* thy pound, which I kept laid up in a napkin:

41 For I feared thee, because thou art an austere man: thou takest up that thou layedst not down, and reapest that thou didst not sow.

42 He saith unto him, Out of thine own mouth will I judge thee, thou wicked servant. Thou knewest that I am an austere man, taking up that I laid not down, and reaping that I did not sow;

43 Then wherefore gavest thou not my money into the bank, and I at my coming should have required it with interest?

44 And he said unto them that stood by, Take away from him the pound, and give it unto him that hath the ten pounds.

45 And they said unto him, Lord, he hath ten pounds.

46 I say unto you, that unto every one that hath shall be given; but from him that hath not, even that which he

"ZACCHEUS, MAKE HASTE AND COME DOWN."

hath shall be taken away from him.

47 Howbeit these mine enemies, which would not that I should reign over them, bring hither, and slay them before me.

48 And when he had thus spoken, he went on before, going up to Jerusalem.

## CHAPTER XLIV.

NOW the passover of the Jews was at hand: and many went up to Jerusalem out of the country before the passover, to purify themselves.

2 They sought therefore for Jesus, and spake one with another, as they stood in the temple, What think ye? That he will not come to the feast?

3 Now the chief priests and the Pharisees had given commandment, that, if any man knew where he was, he should shew it, that they might take him.

### THE LAST WEEK BEFORE THE CRUCIFIXION.

4 Jesus therefore six days before the passover came to Bethany, where Lazarus was, whom Jesus raised from the dead.

5 The common people therefore of the Jews learned that he was there: and they came, not for Jesus' sake only, but that they might see Lazarus also,

6 But the chief priests took counsel that they might put Lazarus also to death;

7 Because that by reason of him many of the Jews went away, and believed on Jesus.

8 Now when Jesus was in Bethany, in the house of Simon the leper,

9 They made him a supper there; and Martha served; but Lazarus was one of them that sat at meat with him.

10 Mary therefore took a pound of ointment of spikenard, very precious, and poured it upon his head, as he sat at meat, and anointed the feet of Jesus, and wiped his feet with her hair:

and the house was filled with the odour of the ointment.

11 But when the disciples saw it, they had indignation, saying, To what purpose is this waste?

12 For this *ointment* might have been sold for much, and given to the poor.

13 And Judas Iscariot, which should betray him, saith,

14 Why was not this ointment sold for three hundred pence, and given to the poor?

15 Now this he said, not because he cared for the poor; but because he was a thief, and having the bag took away what was put therein.

16 But Jesus perceiving it said unto them, Why trouble ye the woman? for she hath wrought a good work upon me.

17 For ye have the poor always with you; but me ye have not always.

18 For in that she poured this ointment upon my body, she did it to prepare me for burial.

19 Verily I say unto you, Wheresoever t h i s gospel shall be preached in the whole world, that also which this woman hath done shall be spoken of for a memorial of her.

April 2, A. D. 30.

20 On the morrow when they draw nigh unto Jerusalem, unto Bethphage and Bethany, at the mount of Olives,

21 A great multitude that had come to the feast, when they heard that Jesus was coming to Jerusalem,

22 Took the branches of the palm trees, and went forth to meet him, and cried out, Hosanna: Blessed *is* he that cometh in the name of the Lord, even the King of Israel.

23 Then Jesus sendeth two of his disciples, and saith unto them, Go your way into the village t h a t is over against you: and straightway as ye enter into it, ye shall find a colt tied, whereon no man ever yet sat; loose him, and bring him.

"WHAT DO YE, LOOSING THE COLT?"

24 And if any one say unto you, Why do ye this? say ye, The Lord hath need of him; and straightway he will send him back hither.

25 And they went away, and found a colt tied at the door without in the open street; and they loose him.

26 And certain of them that stood there said unto them, What do ye, loosing the colt?

27 And they said unto them even as Jesus had said: and they let them go.

28 And they bring the colt unto Jesus, and cast on him their garments; and Jesus sat upon him.

29 Now this is come to pass, that it might be fulfilled which was spoken by the prophet, saying,

30 Tell ye the daughter of Zion,

Behold, thy King cometh unto thee,

Meek, and riding upon an ass,

And upon a colt the foal of an ass.

31 These things understood not his disciples at the first: but when Jesus was glorified, then remembered they that these things were written of him, and that they had done these things unto him.

32 The multitude therefore that was with him when he called Lazarus out of the tomb, and raised him from the dead, bare witness.

33 For this cause also the multitude went and met him, for that they heard that he had done this sign.

34 And the most part of the multitude spread their garments in the way; and others cut branches from the trees, and spread them in the way.

35 And as he was now drawing nigh, *even* at the descent of the mount of Olives, the whole multitude of the disciples began to rejoice and praise God with a loud voice for all the mighty works which they had seen;

36 Saying, Blessed *is* the

King that cometh in the name of the Lord: peace in heaven, and glory in the highest.

37 Blessed *is* the kingdom that cometh, *the kingdom* of our father David: Hosanna in the highest.

38 The Pharisees therefore said among themselves, Behold how ye prevail nothing: lo, the world is gone after him.

39 And some of the Pharisees from the multitude said unto him, Master, rebuke thy disciples.

40 And he answered and said, I tell you that, if these shall hold their peace, the stones will cry out.

41 And when he drew nigh, he saw the city and wept over it, saying,

42 If thou hadst known in this day, even thou, the things which belong unto peace! but now they are hid from thine eyes.

43 For the days shall come upon thee, when thine enemies shall cast up a bank about thee, and compass thee round, and keep thee in on every side,

44 And shall dash thee to the ground, and thy children within thee; and they shall not leave in thee one stone upon another; because thou knewest not the time of thy visitation.

45 And when he was come into Jerusalem, all the city was stirred, saying, Who is this?

THE TEMPLE PURGED.

46 And Jesus entered into the temple of God, and cast out all them that sold and bought in the temple, and overthrew the tables of the money - changers, and the seats of them that sold the doves;

47 And he would not suffer that any man should carry a vessel through the temple.

48 And he taught and said unto them, Is it not written, My house shall be called a house of prayer for all the nations? but ye have made it a den of robbers.

THE TRIUMPHAL ENTRY.

49 And he was teaching daily in the temple. But the chief priests and the scribes and the principal men of the people sought to destroy him:

50 And they could not find what they might do; for the people all hung upon him, listening.

51 And the blind and the lame came to him in the temple: and he healed them.

52 But when the chief priests and the scribes saw the wonderful things that he did, and the children that were crying in the temple and saying, Hosanna to the son of David; they were moved with indignation,

53 And said unto him, Hearest thou what these are saying? And Jesus saith unto them, Yea: did ye never read, Out of the mouth of babes and sucklings thou hast perfected praise?

54 And when he had looked round about upon all things, it being now even-tide, he went out unto Bethany with the twelve.

## CHAPTER XLV.

NOW in the morning as he returned to the city, from Bethany, he hungered.

2 And seeing a fig tree afar off having leaves, he came, if haply he might find anything thereon: and when he came to it, he found nothing but leaves; for it was not the season of figs.

3 And he saith unto it, Let there be no fruit from thee henceforward for ever. And his disciples heard it.

4 And immediately the fig tree withered away.

5 And when he was come into the temple, the chief priests and the elders of the people came unto him as he was teaching, and said, By what authority doest thou these things? and who gave thee.this authority?

6 And Jesus answered and said unto them, I also will ask you one question, which if ye tell me, I likewise will

tell you by what authority I do these things.

7 The baptism of John, whence was it? from heaven or from men? And they reasoned with themselves, saying, If we shall say, From heaven; he will say unto us, Why then did ye not believe him?

8 But should we say, From men—t h e y f e a r e d t h e people: for all verily held John to be a prophet.

9 A n d t h e y answered Jesus and say, We know not. And Jesus saith unto them, Neither tell I you by what authority I do these things.

10 But what think ye? A man had two sons; and he came to the first, and said, Son, go work to-day in the vineyard.

11 And he answered and said, I will not: but afterward he repented himself and went.

12 And he came to the second, and said likewise. And he answered and said, I *go*, sir: and went not.

13 Whether of the twain did the will of his father? They say, The first. Jesus saith unto them, Verily I say unto you, that the publicans and the harlots go into the kingdom of God before you.

14 For John came unto you in the way of righteousness, and ye believed him not: but the publicans and the harlots believed him: and ye, when ye saw it, did not even repent yourselves afterward, that ye might believe him.

THE WICKED HUSBANDMEN.

15 Hear another parable: There was a man that was a householder, which planted a vineyard, and set a hedge about it, and digged a winepress in it, and built a tower, and let it out to husbandmen, and went into another country.

16 And when the season of the fruits drew near, he sent his servants to the husbandmen, to receive his fruits.

17 And the husbandmen took his servants, and beat

The World in Disarray

one, and killed another, and stoned another.

18 Again, he sent other servants more than the first: and they did unto them in like manner.

19 But afterward he sent unto them his beloved son, saying, They will reverence my son.

20 But the husbandmen, when they saw the son, said among themselves, This is the heir; come, let us kill him, and take his inheritance.

21 And they took him, and cast him forth out of the vineyard, and killed him.

22 When therefore the lord of the vineyard shall come, what will he do unto those husbandmen?

23 They say unto him, He will miserably destroy those miserable men, and will let out the vineyard unto other husbandmen, which shall render him the fruits in their seasons.

24 Jesus saith unto them, Did ye never read in the scriptures,

The stone which the builders rejected,

The same was made the head of the corner:

This was from the Lord,

And it is marvellous in our eyes?

25 Therefore say I unto you, The kingdom of God shall be taken away from you, and shall be given to a nation bringing forth the fruits thereof.

26 And he that falleth on this stone shall be broken to pieces: but on whomsoever it shall fall, it will scatter him as dust.

27 And when the chief priests and the Pharisees heard his parables, they perceived that he spake of them.

28 And when they sought to lay hold on him, they feared the multitudes because they took him for a prophet.

29 Then went the Pharisees, and took counsel how

they might ensnare him in *his* talk.

30 For though he had done so many signs before them, yet they believed not on him:

31 That the word of Isaiah the prophet might be fulfilled, which he spake,

Lord who hath believed our report?

And to whom hath the arm of the Lord been revealed?

32 For this cause they could not believe, for that Isaiah said again,

33 He hath blinded their eyes, and he hardened their heart;

Lest they should see with their eyes, and perceive with their heart,

And should turn,

And I should heal them.

34 These things said Isaiah, because he saw his glory; and he spake of him.

35 Nevertheless even of the rulers many believed on him; but because of the Pharisees they did not con-

fess *it*, lest they should be put out of the synagogue:

36 For they loved the glory of men more than the glory of God.

37 And every day he was teaching in the temple; and every night he went out, and lodged in the mount that is called *the mount* of Olives.

## CHAPTER XLVI.

### THE BARREN FIG-TREE.

April 4, A. D. 30.

AND as they pased by in the morning, they saw the fig tree withered away from the roots.

2 And Peter calling to remembrance saith unto him, Rabbi, behold, the fig tree which thou cursedst is withered away.

3 And Jesus answering saith unto them, Have faith in God.

4 Verily I say unto you, Whosoever shall say unto this mountain, Be thou taken up and cast into the sea; and shall not doubt in his heart, but shall believe that what

he saith cometh to pass; he shall have it.

5 Therefore I s a y unto you, All things whatsoever ye pray and ask for, believe that ye have received them, and ye shall have them.

6 A n d whensoever y e stand praying, forgive, if ye have aught against any one; that your Father also which is in heaven may forgive you your trespasses.[1]

7 Now there were certain Greeks among those that went up to worship at the feast:

8 These therefore came to Philip, which was of Bethsaida of Galilee, and asked him, saying, Sir, we would see Jesus.

9 Philip cometh and telleth A n d r e w : A n d r e w cometh, and Philip, and they tell Jesus.

10 And Jesus answereth them, saying, The hour is

come, that the Son of man should be glorified.

11 Verily, verily, I say unto you, Except a grain of wheat fall into the earth and die, i t abideth b y itself alone; but if it die, it beareth much fruit.

12 He that loveth his life loseth it; and he that hateth his life in this world shall keep it unto life eternal.

13 If any man serve me, let him follow me; and where I am, there shall also my servant be: if any man serve me, h i m w i l l the Father honour.

14 Now is my soul troubled; and what shall I say? Father, save me from this hour. But for this cause came I unto this hour.

A VOICE FROM HEAVEN.

15 Father, glorify t h y name. There came therefore a voice out of heaven, *saying*, I have both glorified it, and will glorify it again.

16 The multitude therefore, that stood b y, a n d heard it, said that it had

---

[1] Many ancient authorities add: *But if ye do not forgive, neither will your Father which is in heaven forgive your trespasses.*

thundered: others said, An angel hath spoken to him.

17 Jesus answered and said, This voice hath not come for my sake, but for your sakes.

18 Now is the judgement of this world: now shall the prince of this world be cast out.

19 And I, if I be lifted up from the earth, will draw all men unto myself.

20 But this he said, signifying by what manner of death he should die.

21 The multitude therefore answered him, We have heard out of the law that the Christ abideth for ever: and how sayest thou, The Son of man must be lifted up? who is this Son of man?

22 Jesus therefore said unto them, Yet a little while is the light among you. Walk while ye have the light, that darkness overtake you not: and he that walketh in the darkness knoweth not whither he goeth.

23 While ye have the light, believe on the light, that ye may become sons of light.

24 And Jesus cried and said, He that believeth on me, believeth not on me, but on him that sent me.

25 And he that beholdeth me beholdeth him that sent me.

26 I am come a light into the world, that whosoever believeth on me may not abide in the darkness.

27 And if any man hear my sayings, and keep them not, I judge him not: for I came not to judge the world, but to save the world.

28 He that rejecteth me, and receiveth not my sayings, hath one that judgeth him: the word that I spake, the same shall judge him in the last day.

29 For I spake not from myself; but the Father which sent me, he hath given me a commandment, what I should say, and what I should speak.

30 And I know that his commandment is life eter-

"I am Come a Light Into the World."

nal: the things therefore which I speak, even as the Father hath said unto me, so I speak.

31 And he sat down over against the treasury, and beheld how the multitude cast money into the treasury: and many that were rich cast in much.

### THE POOR WIDOW.

32 And there came a poor widow, and she cast in two mites, which make a farthing.

33 And he called unto him his disciples, and said unto them, Verily I say unto you, this poor widow cast in more than all they which are casting into the treasury:

34 For they all did cast in of their superfluity; but she of her want did cast in all that she had, *even* all her living.

## CHAPTER XLVII.

### THE MARRIAGE FEAST.

AND Jesus answered and spake again in parables unto them, saying,

2 The kingdom of heaven is likened unto a certain king, which made a marriage feast for his son,

3 And sent forth his servants to call them that were bidden to the marriage feast: and they would not come.

4 Again he sent forth other servants, saying, Tell them that are bidden, Behold, I have made ready my dinner: my oxen and my fatlings are killed, and all things are ready: come to the marriage feast.

5 But they made light of it, and went their ways, one to his own farm, another to his merchandise:

6 And the rest laid hold on his servants, and entreated them shamefully, and killed them.

7 But the king was wroth: and he sent forth his armies, and destroyed those murderers, and burned their city.

'8 Then saith he to his servants, The wedding is ready, but they that were bidden were not worthy.

9 Go ye therefore unto the partings of the highways, and as many as ye shall find, bid to the marriage feast.

10 And those servants went out into the highways, and gathered together all as many as they found, both bad and good: and the wedding was filled with guests.

11 But when the king came in to behold the guests, he saw there a man which had not on a wedding-garment:

12 And he saith unto him, Friend, how camest thou in hither not having a wedding garment? And he was speechless.

13 Then the king said to the servants, Bind him hand and foot, and cast him out into the outer darkness; and there shall be the weeping and gnashing of teeth.

14 For many are called, but few chosen.

CÆSAR'S TRIBUTE MONEY.

15 Then went the Phari-

sees, and took counsel how they might ensnare him in *his* talk.

16 And they sent to him their disciples, with the Herodians, saying, Master, we know that thou art true, and teachest the way of God in truth, and carest not for any one: for thou regardest not the person of men.

17 Tell us therefore, What thinkest thou? Is it lawful to give tribute unto Cæsar, or not?

18 But Jesus perceived their wickedness, and said, Why tempt ye me, ye hypocrites?

19 Shew me the tribute money. And they brought unto him a penny.

20 And he saith unto them, Whose is this image and superscription?

21 They say unto him, Cæsar's. Then saith he unto them, Render therefore unto Cæsar the things that are Cæsar's; and unto God the things that are God's.

22 And when they heard

" THE TRIBUTE MONEY."

it, they marvelled and left him, and went their way.

23 On that day there came to him Sadducees, which say that there is no resurrection: and they asked him, saying,

24 Master, Moses said, If a man die, having no children, his brother shall marry his wife, and raise up seed unto his brother.

25 Now there were with us seven brethren: and the first married and deceased, and having no seed left his wife unto his brother;

26 And the second took her, and died, leaving no seed behind him; and the third likewise: and the seven left no seed.

27 Last of all the woman also died.

28 In the resurrection whose wife shall she be of them? for the seven had her to wife.

29 Jesus said unto them, Is it not for this cause that ye err, that ye know not the scriptures, nor the power of God?

30 The sons of this world marry, and are given in marriage:

31 But they that are accounted worthy to attain to that world, and the resurrection from the dead, neither marry, nor are given in marriage:

32 Neither can they die any more: for they are equal unto the angels; and are sons of God, being sons of the resurrection.

33 But that the dead are raised, even Moses shewed, in *the place concerning* the Bush, when he calleth the Lord the God of Abraham, and the God of Isaac, and the God of Jacob.

34 Now he is not the God of the dead, but of the living: for all live unto him.

35 Ye do greatly err.

36 And when the multitudes heard it, they were astonished at his teaching.

37 And certain of the scribes answering said, Master, thou hast well said.

38 But the Pharisees,

when they heard that he had put the Sadducees to silence, gathered themselves together.

39 And one of them, a lawyer, asked him a question, tempting him.

40 Master, which is the great commandment in the law?

41 And he said unto him, Thou shalt love the Lord thy God with all thy heart, and with all thy soul, and with all thy mind.

42 This is the great and first commandment.

43 And a second like *unto it* is this, Thou shalt love thy neighbour as thyself.

44 On these two commandments hangeth the whole law, and the prophets.

45 And the scribe said unto him, Of a truth, Master, thou hast well said that he is one; and there is none other but he:

46 And to love him with all the heart, and with all the understanding, and with all the strength, and to love his neighbour as himself, is much more than all whole burnt offerings and sacrifices.

47 And when Jesus saw that he answered discreetly, he said unto him, Thou art not far from the kingdom of God. And no man after that durst ask him any question.

48 Now while the Pharisees were gathered together, Jesus asked them a question, saying,

49 What think ye of the Christ? whose son is he? They say unto him, *The son* of David.

50 He saith unto them, How then doth David in the spirit call him Lord,

51 For David himself saith in the book of Psalms,

The Lord said unto my Lord,

Sit thou on my right hand,

52 Till I make thine enemies the footstool of thy feet.

53 If David then calleth him Lord, how is he his son?

54 And no one was able

to answer him a word, neither durst any man from that day forth ask him any more questions.

55 And the common people heard him gladly.

## CHAPTER XLVIII.

THEN spake Jesus to the multitudes and to his disciples, saying,

2 The scribes and the Pharisees sit on Moses' seat:

3 All things therefore whatsoever they bid you, *these* do and observe: but do not ye after their works; for they say, and do not.

4 Yea, they bind heavy burdens and grievous to be borne, and lay them on men's shoulders; but they themselves will not move them with their finger.

5 But all their works they do for to be seen of men: for they make broad their phylacteries and enlarge the borders *of their garments,*

6 And love the chief place at feasts, and the chief seats in the synagogues, and the salutations in the marketplaces, and to be called of men, Rabbi.

7 But be not ye called Rabbi: for one is your teacher, and all ye are brethren.

8 And call no man your father on the earth: for one is your Father, which is in heaven.

9 Neither be ye called masters: for one is your master, *even* the Christ.

10 But he that is greatest among you shall be your servant.

11 And whosoever shall exalt himself shall be humbled; and whosoever shall humble himself shall be exalted.

WOE UNTO YOU, PHARISEES.

12 But woe unto you, scribes and Pharisees, hypocrites! because ye shut the kingdom of heaven against men: for ye enter not in yourselves, neither suffer ye them that are entering in to enter.

13 Woe unto you, scribes

and Pharisees, hypocrites! for ye compass sea and land to make one proselyte; and when he is become so, ye make him twofold more a son of hell than yourselves.

14 Woe unto you, ye blind guides, which say, Whosoever shall swear by the temple, it is nothing; but whosoever shall swear by the gold of the temple, he is a debtor.

15 Ye fools and blind: for whether is greater, the gold, or the temple that hath sanctified the gold?

16 And, Whosoever shall swear by the altar, it is nothing; but w h o s o e v e r shall swear by the gift that is upon it, he is a debtor.

17 Ye blind: for whether is greater, the gift, or the altar that santifieth the gift?

18 H e therefore t h a t sweareth b y t h e altar, sweareth by it, and by all things thereon.

19 And he that sweareth by the temple, sweareth by it, and by him that dwelleth therein.

20 And he that sweareth by the heaven, sweareth by the throne of God, and by him that sitteth thereon.

21 Woe unto you, scribes and Pharisees, hypocrites! for ye tithe mint and anise and cummin, and have left undone the weightier matters of the law, judgement, and mercy, and faith: but these ye ought to have done, and not to have left the other undone.

22 Ye blind guides, which strain out the gnat, and swallow the camel.

23 Woe unto you, scribes and Pharisees, hypocrites! for ye cleanse the outside of the cup and of the platter, but within they are full from extortion and excess.

24 Thou blind Pharisee, cleanse first the inside of the cup and of the platter, that the outside thereof may become clean also.

25 Woe unto you, scribes and Pharisees, hypocrites! for ye are like unto whited sepulchres, which outwardly

"The Scribes and the Pharisees Sit on Moses' Seat."

appear beautiful, but inwardly are full of dead men's bones, and of all uncleanness.

26 Even so ye also outwardly appear righteous unto men, but inwardly ye are full of hypocrisy and iniquity.

27 Woe unto you, scribes and Pharisees, hypocrites! for ye build the sepulchres of the prophets, and garnish the tombs of the righteous,

28 And say, If we had been in the days of our fathers, we should not have been partakers with them in the blood of the prophets.

29 Wherefore ye witness to yourselves, that ye are sons of them that slew the prophets.

30 Fill ye up then the measure of your fathers.

31 Ye serpents, ye offspring of vipers, how shall ye escape the judgement of hell?

32 Therefore, behold, I send unto you prophets, and wise men, and scribes: some of them shall ye kill and crucify; and some of them shall ye scourge in your synagogues, and persecute from city to city:

33 That upon you may come all the righteous blood shed on the earth, from the blood of Abel the righteous unto the blood of Zachariah son of Barachiah, whom ye slew between the sanctuary and the altar.

34 Verily I say unto you, All these things shall come upon this generation.

35 O Jerusalem, Jerusalem, which killeth the prophets, and stoneth them that are sent unto her! how often would I have gathered thy children together, even as a hen gathereth her chickens under her wings, and ye would not!

36 Behold, your house is left unto you desolate.

37 For I say unto you, Ye shall not see me henceforth, till ye shall say, Blessed *is* he that cometh in the name of the Lord.

## CHAPTER XLIX.

### THE DOOM OF JERUSALEM.

AND Jesus went out from the temple, and was going on his way; and his disciples came to him to shew him the buildings of the temple.

2 But he answered and said unto them, See ye not all these things? verily I say unto you, There shall not be left here one stone upon another, that shall not be thrown down.

3 And as he sat on the mount of Olives, the disciples came unto him privately, saying, Tell us, when shall these things be? and what *shall be* the sign of thy coming, and of the end of the world?

4 And Jesus answered and said unto them, Take heed that no man lead you astray.

5 For many shall come in my name, saying, I am the Christ; and shall lead many astray.

6 The time is at hand: go ye not after them.

7 And when ye shall hear of wars and tumults, be not terrified: for these things must needs come to pass first; but the end is not immediately.

8 For nation shall rise against nation, and kingdom against kingdom:

9 And there shall be great earthquakes, and in divers places famines and pestilences; and there shall be terrors and great signs from heaven.

10 But all these things are the beginning of travail.

11 But take ye heed to yourselves: for they shall deliver you up to councils; and in synagogues shall ye be beaten;

12 And before governors and kings shall ye stand for my sake, for a testimony unto them.

13 Ye shall be delivered up even by parents, and brethren, and kinsfolk, and friends; and *some* of you shall they cause to be put to death.

14 And ye shall be hated of all men for my name's sake.

15 But not a hair of your head shall perish.

16 In your patience ye shall win your souls.

17 And when they lead you *to judgement,* and deliver you up, be not anxious beforehand what ye shall speak: but whatsoever shall be given you in that hour, that speak ye: for it is not ye that speak, but the Holy Ghost.

18 Settle it therefore in your hearts, not to meditate beforehand how to answer:

19 For I will give you a mouth and wisdom, which all your adversaries shall not be able to withstand or to gainsay.

20 And then shall many stumble, and shall deliver up one another, and shall hate one another.

21 And many false prophets shall arise, and shall lead many astray.

22 And because iniquity shall be multiplied, the love of the many shall wax cold.

23 But he that endureth to the end, the same shall be saved.

24 And this gospel of the kingdom shall be preached in the whole world for a testimony unto all the nations; and then shall the end come.

25 When therefore ye see the abomination of desolation, which was spoken of by Daniel the prophet, standing in the holy place (let him that readeth understand),

26 When ye see Jerusalem compassed with armies, then know that her desolation is at hand.

27 Then let them that are in Judæa flee unto the mountains:

28 And let them that are in the midst of her depart out; and let not them that are in the country enter therein.

29 Let him that is on the housetop not go down to take out the things that are in his house:

30 And let him that is in the field not return back to take nis cloke.

31 For these are days of vengeance, that all things which are written may be fulfilled.

32 Woe unto them that are with child and to them that give suck in those days! for there shall be great distress upon the land, and wrath unto this people.

33 And they shall fall by the edge of the sword, and shall be led captive into all the nations: and Jerusalem shall be trodden down of the Gentiles, until the times of the Gentiles be fulfilled.

34 And pray ye that it be not in the winter.

35 For those days shall be tribulation, such as there hath not been the like from the beginning of the creation which God created until now, and never shall be.

36 And except the Lord had shortened the days, no flesh would have been saved: but for the elect's sake, whom he chose, he shortened the days.

37 And then if any man shall say unto you, Lo, here is the Christ; or, Lo, there;

38 Believe *it* not: for there shall arise false Christs and false prophets, and shall shew signs and wonders, that they may lead astray, if possible, the elect.

39 Behold, I have told you all things beforehand.

40 If therefore they shall say unto you, Behold, he is in the wilderness; go not forth: Behold, he is in the inner chambers; believe *it* not.

41 For as the lightning cometh forth from the east, and is seen even unto the west; so shall be the coming of the Son of man.

42 Wheresoever the carcase is, there will the eagles be gathered together.

## CHAPTER L.

IMMEDIATELY, after the tribulation of those days, the sun shall be darkened,

Jesus Weeping Over Jerusalem.

and the moon shall not give her light, and the stars shall fall from heaven, and the powers of the heavens shall be shaken:

2 And upon the earth distress of nations, in perplexity for the roaring of the sea and the billows;

3 Men fainting for fear, and for expectation of the things which are coming on the world: for the powers of the heavens shall be shaken.

4 And then shall appear the sign of the Son of man in heaven: and then shall all the tribes of the earth mourn, and they shall see the Son of man coming on the clouds of heaven with power and great glory.

5 And he shall send forth his angels with a great sound of a trumpet, and they shall gather together his elect from the four winds, from one end of heaven to the other.

6 From the uttermost part of the earth to the uttermost part of heaven.

7 But when these things begin to come to pass, look up, and lift up your heads; because your redemption draweth nigh.

8 And he spake to them a parable: Behold the fig tree, and all the trees:

9 When they now shoot forth, ye see it and know of your own selves that the summer is now nigh.

10 Even so ye also, when ye see these things coming to pass, know ye that the kingdom of God is nigh, *even* at the doors.

11 Verily I say unto you, This generation shall not pass away, until all these things be accomplished.

12 Heaven and earth shall pass away: but my words shall not pass away.

13 But take heed to yourselves, lest haply your hearts be overcharged with surfeiting, and drunkenness, and cares 'of this life, and that day come on you suddenly as a snare.

14 For *so* shall it come

upon all them that dwell on the face of all the earth.

15 But watch ye at every season, making supplication, that ye may prevail to escape all these things that shall come to pass, and to stand before the Son of man.

16 But of that day or that hour knoweth no one, not even the angels in heaven, neither the Son, but the Father.

17 And as *were* the days of Noah, so shall be the coming of the Son of man.

18 For as in those days which were before the flood they were eating and drinking, marrying and giving in marriage, until the day that Noah entered into the ark,

19 And they knew not until the flood came, and took them all away; so shall be the coming of the Son of man.

20 Then shall two men be in the field; one is taken, and one is left:

21 Two women *shall be* grinding at the mill; one is taken, and one is left.

22 Take ye heed, watch and pray; for ye know not when the time is.

23 *It is* as *when* a man, sojourning in another country, having left his house, and given authority to his servants, to each one his work, commanded also the porter to watch.

24 Who then is the faithful and wise servant, whom his lord hath set over his household, to give them their food in due season?

25 Blessed is that servant, whom his lord when he cometh shall find so doing.

26 Verily I say unto you that he will set him over all that he hath.

27 But if that evil servant shall say in his heart, My lord tarrieth;

28 And shall begin to beat his fellow-servants, and shall eat and drink with the drunken;

29 The lord of that servant shall come in a day when he

"... SED IS THAT SERVANT, WHOM HIS LORD, WHEN HE COMETH SHALL FIND SO DOING."

expecteth not, and in an hour when he knoweth not,

30 And s h a l l cut him asunder, and appoint his portion with the hypocrites: there shall be the weeping and gnashing of teeth.

31 Watch therefore: for ye know not when the lord of t h e h o u s e cometh, whether at even, or at midnight, or at cockcrowing, or in the morning;

32 Lest coming suddenly he find you sleeping.

33 And what I say unto you I say unto all, Watch.

## CHAPTER LI.

### THE TEN VIRGINS.

THEN shall the kingdom of heaven be likened unto ten virgins, which took their lamps, and went forth to meet the bridegroom.

2 And five of them were foolish, and five were wise.

3 For the foolish, when they took their lamps, took no oil with them:

4 But the wise took oil in their vessels w i t h their lamps.

5 Now while the bridegroom tarried, they all slumbered and slept.

6 But at midnight there is a cry, Behold, the bridegroom! Come ye forth to meet him.

7 Then all those virgins arose, and trimmed their lamps.

8 And the foolish said unto the wise, Give us of your oil; for our lamps are going out.

9 But the wise answered, saying, Peradventure there will not be enough for us and you: go ye rather to them that sell, and buy for yourselves.

10 And while they went away to buy, the bridegroom came; and they that were ready went in with him to the marriage feast: and the door was shut.

11 Afterward come also the other virgins, saying, Lord, Lord, open to us.

12 But he answered and

said, Verily I say unto you, I know you not.

13 Watch therefore, for ye know not the day nor the hour.

USED AND MISUSED TALENTS.

14 For *it is* as *when* a man, going into another country, called his own servants, and delivered unto them his goods.

15 And unto one he gave five talents, to another two, to another one; to each according to his several ability; and he went on his journey.

16 Straightway he that received the five talents went and traded with them, and made other five talents.

17 In like manner he also that *received* the two gained other two.

18 But he that received the one went away and digged in the earth, and hid his lord's money.

19 Now after a long time the lord of those servants cometh, and maketh a reckoning with them.

20 And he that received the five talents came and brought other five talents, saying, Lord, thou deliveredst unto me five talents: lo, I have gained other five talents.

21 His lord said unto him, Well done, good and faithful servant: t h o u hast been faithful over a few things, I will set thee over many things: enter thou into the joy of thy lord.

22 And he also that *received* the two talents came and said, Lord, thou deliveredst unto me two talents: lo, I have gained other two talents.

23 His lord said unto him, Well done, good and faithful servant; thou hast been faithful over a few things, I will set thee over many things: enter thou into the joy of thy lord.

24 And he also that had received the one talent came and said, Lord, I knew thee that thou art a hard man, reaping where thou didst not

At Midnight There is a Cry, 'Behold, the Bridegroom.'

sow, and gathering where thou didst not scatter:

25 And I was afraid, and went away and hid thy talent in the earth: lo, thou hast thine own.

26 But his lord answered and said unto him, Thou wicked and slothful servant, thou knewest that I reap where I sowed not, and gather where I did not scatter;

27 Thou oughtest therefore to have put my money to the bankers, and at my coming I should have received back mine own with interest.

28 Take ye away therefore the talent from him, and give it unto him that hath the ten talents.

29 For unto every one that hath shall be given, and he shall have abundance: but from him that hath not, even that which he hath shall be taken away.

30 And cast ye out the unprofitable servant into the outer darkness: there shall be the weeping and gnashing of teeth.

31 But when the Son of man shall come in his glory, and all the angels with him, then shall he sit on the throne of his glory:

32 And before him shall be gathered all the nations: and he shall separate them one from another, as the shepherd separateth the sheep from the goats:

33 And he shall set the sheep on his right hand, but the goats on the left.

34 Then shall the King say unto them on his right hand, Come, ye blessed of my Father, inherit the kingdom prepared for you from the foundation of the world:

35 For I was an hungred, and ye gave me meat: I was thirsty, and ye gave me drink: I was a stranger, and ye took me in;

36 Naked, and ye clothed me: I was sick, and ye visited me: I was in prison, and ye came unto me.

37 Then shall the right-

cous answer him, saying, Lord, when saw we thee an hungred, and fed thee? or athirst, and gave thee drink?

38 And when saw we thee a stranger, and took thee in? or naked, and clothed thee?

39 And when saw we thee sick, or in prison, and came unto thee?

40 And the King shall answer and say unto them, Verily I say unto you, Inasmuch as ye did it unto one of these my brethren, *even* these least, ye did it unto me.

41 Then shall he say also unto them on the left hand, Depart from me, ye cursed, into the eternal fire which is prepared for the devil and his angels:

42 For I was an hungred, and ye gave me no meat: I was thirsty, and ye gave me no drink:

43 I was a stranger, and ye took me not in; naked, and ye clothed me not; sick, and in prison, and ye visited me not.

44 Then shall they also answer, saying, Lord, when saw we thee an hungred, or athirst, or a stranger, or naked, or sick, or in prison, and did not minister unto thee?

45 Then shall he answer them, saying, Verily I say unto you, Inasmuch as ye did it not unto one of these least, ye did it not unto me.

46 And these shall go away into eternal punishment: but the righteous into eternal life.

## CHAPTER LII.
### April 6, A. D. 30.

AND it came to pass, when Jesus had finished all these words, he said unto his disciples,

2 Ye know that after two days the passover cometh, and the Son of man is delivered up to be crucified.

3 Then were gathered together the chief priests, and the elders of the people, unto the court of the high priest, who was called Caiaphas;

4 And they took counsel

JUDAS AND THE PRIESTS.

together that they might take Jesus by subtilty, and kill him.

5 But they said, Not during the feast, lest a tumult arise among the people; for they feared the people.

6 And Satan entered into Judas who was called Iscariot, being of the number of the twelve.

7 And he went away, and communed with the chief priests and captains, how he might deliver him unto them.

8 And said, What are ye willing to give me, and I will deliver him unto you?

9 And they were glad, and covenanted to g i v e him money.

10 And they weighed unto him thirty pieces of silver.

11 And from that time he sought opportunity to deliver him *unto them*, in the absence of the multitude.

THE LORD'S SUPPER.

12 Now on the first *day* of unleavened bread the disciples came to Jesus, saying,

Where wilt thou that we make ready for thee to eat the passover?

13 And he sent Peter and John, saying, Go and make ready for us the passover, that we may eat.

14 And they said unto him, Where wilt thou that we make ready?

15 And he said unto them, Behold, when ye are entered into the city, there shall meet you a man bearing a pitcher of water; follow him into the house whereinto he goeth.

16 And ye shall say unto the goodman of the house, The Master saith unto thee,

17 My time is at hand; I keep the passover at thy house.

18 Where is the guestchamber, where I shall eat the passover with my disciples?

19 And he will shew you a large upper room furnished: there make ready.

20 And they went, and found as he had said unto

them: and they made ready the passover.

### WASHING HIS DISCIPLES' FEET.

21 Now before the feast of the passover, Jesus knowing that his hour was come that he should depart out of this world unto the Father, having loved his own which were in the world, he loved them unto the end.

22 And when the hour was come, he sat down, and the apostles with him.

23 And he said unto them, With desire I have desired to eat this passover with you before I suffer:

24 For I say unto you, I will not eat it, until it be fulfilled in the kingdom of God.

25 And he received a cup, and when he had given thanks, he said, Take this, and divide it among yourselves:

26 For I say unto you, I will not drink from henceforth of the fruit of the vine, until the kingdom of God shall come.

27 And there arose also a contention a m o n g them, which of them is accounted to be greatest.

28 And he said unto them, the kings of the Gentiles have lordship over them; and they that have authority over them are called Benefactors.

29 But ye *shall* not *be* so: but he that is the greater among you, let him become as the younger; and he that is chief, as he that doth serve.

30 For whether is greater, he that sitteth at meat, or he that serveth? is not he that sitteth at meat? but I am in the midst of you as he that serveth.

31 But ye are they which have continued with me in my temptations;

32 And I appoint unto you a kingdom, even as my Father appointed unto me,

33 That ye may eat and drink at my table in my kingdom; and ye shall sit on thrones judging the twelve tribes of Israel.

THE LAST SUPPER.

34 And during supper, the devil having already put into the heart of Judas Iscariot, Simon's *son*, to betray him,

35 *Jesus*, knowing that the Father had given all things into his hands, and that he came forth from God, and goeth unto God, riseth from supper,

36 And layeth aside his garments; and he took a towel, and girded himself.

37 Then he poureth water into the bason, and began to wash the disciples' feet, and to wipe them with the towel wherewith he was girded.

38 So he cometh to Simon Peter. He saith unto him, Lord, dost thou wash my feet?

39 Jesus answered and said unto him, What I do thou knowest not now; but thou shalt understand hereafter.

40 Peter saith unto him, Thou shalt never wash my feet. Jesus answered him, If I wash thee not, thou hast no part with me.

41 Simon Peter saith unto him, Lord, not my feet only, but also my hands and my head.

42 Jesus saith to him, He that is bathed needeth not save to wash his feet, but is clean every whit: and ye are clean, but not all.

43 For he knew him that should betray him; therefore said he, Ye are not all clean.

44 So when he had washed their feet, and taken his garments, and sat down again, he said unto them, Know ye what I have done to you?

45 Ye call me, Master, and, Lord: and ye say well; for so I am.

46 If I then, the Lord and the Master, have washed your feet, ye also ought to wash one another's feet.

47 For I have given you an example, that ye also should do as I have done to you.

48 Verily, verily, I say unto you, A servant is not

greater than his lord; neither one that is sent greater than he that sent him.

49 If ye know these things, blessed are ye if ye do them.

50 I speak not of you all: I know whom I have chosen: but that the scripture may be fulfilled, He that eateth my bread lifted up his heel against me.

51 From henceforth I tell you before it come to pass, that, when it is come to pass, ye may believe that I am *he*.

52 Verily, verily, I say unto you, He that receiveth whomsoever I send receiveth me; and he that receiveth me receiveth him that sent me.

### JUDAS.

53 When Jesus had thus said, he was troubled in the spirit, and testified, and said, Verily, verily, I say unto you, that one of you shall betray me.

54 Behold, the hand of him that betrayeth me is with me on the table.

55 And they began to question among themselves which of them it was that should do this thing.

56 And they were exceeding sorrowful, and began to say unto him every one, Is it I, Lord?

57 And he answered and said, He that dipped his hand with me in the dish, the same shall betray me.

58 The Son of man goeth, even as it is written of him: but w o e unto that man through whom the Son of man is betrayed! good were it for that man if he had not been born.

59 The disciples looked one on another, doubting of whom he spake.

60 There was at the table reclining in Jesus' bosom one of his disciples, whom Jesus loved.

61 Simon Peter therefore beckoneth to him, and saith unto him, Tell *us* who is it of whom he speaketh.

62 He leaning back, as he was, on Jesus' breast saith unto him, Lord, who is it?

THE DISCIPLE WHOM JESUS LOVED

63 Jesus therefore answereth, He it is, for whom I shall dip the sop, and give it him. So when he had dipped the sop, he taketh and giveth it to Judas, *the son* of Simon Iscariot.

64 And Judas, which betrayed him, answered and said, Is it I, Rabbi? He saith unto him, Thou hast said.

65 And after the sop, then entered Satan into him. Jesus therefore saith unto him, That thou doest, do quickly.

66 Now no man at the table knew for what intent he spake this unto him.

67 For some thought, because Judas had the bag, that Jesus said unto him, Buy what things we have need of for the feast; or that he should give something to the poor.

68 He then having received the sop went out straightway: and it was night.

69 When therefore he was gone out, Jesus saith, Now is the Son of man glorified, and God is glorified in him;

70 And God shall glorify him in himself, and straightway shall he glorify him.

71 Little children, yet a little while I am with you. Ye shall seek me: and as I said unto the Jews, Whither I go, ye cannot come; so now I say unto you.

72 A new commandment I give unto you, that ye love one another; even as I have loved you, that ye also love one another.

73 By this shall all men know that ye are my disciples, if ye have love one to another.

74 Simon Peter saith unto him, Lord, whither goest thou? Jesus answered, Whither I go, thou canst not follow me now; but thou shalt follow afterwards.

75 Peter saith unto him, Lord, why cannot I follow thee even now? I will lay down my life for thee.

76 Jesus answereth, Wilt thou lay down thy life for

me? Verily, verily, I say unto thee, The cock shall not crow, till thou hast denied me thrice.

77 And as they were eating, Jesus took bread, and blessed, and brake it; and he gave to his disciples, and said, Take, eat; this is my body. This do in remembrance of me.

78 And he took a cup, and gave thanks, and gave to them, saying, Drink ye all of it; and they all drank of it.

79 And he said unto them. This is my blood of the covenant, which is shed for many, unto remission of sins.

80 But I say unto you, I will not drink henceforth of this fruit of the vine, until that day when I drink it new with you in my Father's kingdom.

## CHAPTER LIII.

### THE FAREWELL.

LET not your heart be troubled: ye believe in God, believe also in me.

2 In my Father's house are many mansions; if it were not so, I would have told you; for I go to prepare a place for you.

3 And if I go and prepare a place for you, I come again, and will receive you unto myself; that where I am, *there* ye may be also.

4 And whither I go, ye know the way.

5 Thomas saith unto him, Lord, we know not whither thou goest; how know we the way?

6 Jesus saith unto him, I am the way, and the truth, and the life: no one cometh unto the Father, but by me.

7 If ye had known me, ye would have known my Father also: from henceforth ye know him, and have seen him.

8 Philip saith unto him, Lord, shew us the Father, and it sufficeth us.

9 Jesus saith unto him, Have I been so long time with you, and dost thou not know me, Philip? he that

JUDAS LEAVING THE SUPPER ROOM.

hath seen me hath seen the Father: how sayest thou, Shew us the Father?

10 Believest thou not that I am in the Father, and the Father in me? the words that I say unto you I speak not from myself: but the Father abiding in me doeth his works.

11 Believe me that I am in the Father, and the Father in me: or else believe me for the very works' sake.

12 Verily, verily, I say unto you, He that believeth on me, the works that I do shall he do also; and greater *works* than these shall he do; because I go unto the Father.

13 And whatsoever ye shall ask in my name, that will I do, that the Father may be glorified in the Son.

14 If ye shall ask me anything in my name, that will I do.

15 If ye love me, ye will keep my commandments.

16 And I will pray the Father, and he shall give you another Comforter, that he may be with you forever,

17 *Even* the Spirit of truth: whom the world cannot receive; for it beholdeth him not, neither knoweth him: ye know him; for he abideth with you, and shall be in you.

18 I will not leave you desolate:

19 I come unto you. Yet a little while, and the world beholdeth me no more; but ye behold me: because I live ye shall live also.

20 In that day ye shall know that I am in my Father, and ye in me, and I in you.

21 He that hath my commandments, and keepeth them, he it is that loveth me: and he that loveth me shall be loved of my Father, and I will love him, and will manifest myself unto him.

22 Judas (not Iscariot) saith unto him, Lord, what is come to pass that thou wilt manifest thyself unto us, and not unto the world?

23 Jesus answered and said unto him, If a man love me, he will keep my word; and my Father will love him, and we will come unto him, and make our abode with him.

24 He that loveth me not keepeth not my words: and the word which ye hear is not mine, but the Father's who sent me.

25 These things have I spoken unto you, while *yet* abiding with you.

26 But the Comforter, *even* the Holy Spirit, whom the Father will send in my name, he shall teach you all things, and bring to your remembrance all that I said unto you.

27 Peace I leave with you; my peace I give unto you: not as the world giveth, give I unto you. Let not your heart be troubled, neither let it be fearful.

28 Ye heard how I said to you, I go away, and I come unto you. If ye loved me, ye would have rejoiced, be-cause I go unto the Father: for the Father is greater than I.

29 And now I have told you before it come to pass, that, when it is come to pass, ye may believe.

30 I will no more speak much with you, for the prince of the world cometh:

31 And he hath nothing in me; but that the world may know that I love the Father, and as the Father gave me commandment, even so I do. Arise, let us go hence.

## CHAPTER LIV.

I AM the true vine, and my Father is the husband-man.

2 Every branch in me that beareth not fruit, he taketh it away: and every *branch* that beareth fruit, he cleanseth it, that it may bear more fruit.

3 Already ye are clean be-cause of the word which I have spoken unto you.

4 Abide in me, and I in you. As the branch cannot

" This is My Blood of the Covenant which is Shed for Many."

bear fruit of itself, except it abide in the vine; so neither can ye, except ye abide in me.

5 I am the vine, ye are the branches: He that abideth in me, and I in him, the same beareth much fruit: for apart from me ye can do nothing.

6 If a man abide not in me, he is cast forth as a branch, and is withered; and they gather them, and cast them into the fire, and they are burned.

7 If ye abide in me, and my words abide in you, ask whatsoever ye will, and it shall be done unto you.

8 Herein is my Father glorified, that ye bear much fruit; and *so* shall ye be my disciples.

9 Even as the Father hath loved me, I also have loved you: abide ye in my love.

10 If ye keep my commandments, ye shall abide in my love; even as I have kept my Father's commandments, and abide in his love.

11 These things have I spoken unto you, that my joy may be in you, and *that* your joy may be fulfilled.

12 This is my commandment, that ye love one another, even as I have loved you.

13 Greater love hath no man than this, that a man lay down his life for his friends.

14 Ye are my friends, if ye do the things which I command you.

15 No longer do I call you servants; for the servant knoweth not what his lord doeth: but I have called you friends; for all things that I heard from my Father I have made known unto you.

16 Ye did not choose me, but I chose you, and appointed you, that ye should go and bear fruit, and *that* your fruit should abide: that whatsoever ye shall ask of the Father in my name, he may give it you.

17 These things I command you, that ye may love one another.

18 If the world hateth you, ye know that it hath hated me before *it hated* you.

19 If ye were of the world, the world would love its own: but because ye are not of the world, but I chose you out of the world, therefore the world hateth you.

20 Remember the word that I said unto you, A servant is not greater than his lord. If they persecuted me, they will also persecute you; if they kept my word, they will keep yours also.

21 But all these things will they do unto you for my name's sake, because they know not him that sent me.

22 If I had not come and spoken unto them, they had not had sin: but now they have no excuse for their sin.

23 He that hateth me hateth my Father also.

24 If I had not done among them the works which none other did, they had not had sin: but now have they both seen and hated both me and my Father.

25 But *this cometh to pass*, that the word may be fulfilled that is written in their law, They hated me without a cause.

26 But when the Comforter is come, whom I will send unto you from the Father, *even* the Spirit of truth, w h i c h proceedeth from the Father, he shall bear witness of me:

27 And ye also bear witness, because ye have been with me from the beginning.

### CHAPTER LV.

THESE things have I spoken unto you, that ye should not be made to stumble.

2 They shall put you out of the synagogues: yea, the hour cometh, that whosoever killeth you shall think that he offereth service unto God.

3 And these things will they do, because they have not known the Father, nor me.

4 But these things have I spoken unto you, that when

"When the Comforter is Come, whom I Will Send."

their hour is come, ye may remember them, how that I told you. And these things I said not unto you from the beginning, because I was with you.

5 But now I go unto him that sent me; and none of you asketh me, Whither goest thou?

6 But because I have spoken these things unto you, sorrow hath filled your heart.

7 Nevertheless I tell you the truth; it is expedient for you that I go away: for if I go not away, the Comforter will not come unto you; but if I go, I will send him unto you.

8 And he, when he is come, will convict the world in respect of sin, and of righteousness, and of judgement:

9 Of sin, because they believe not on me;

10 Of righteousness, because I go to the Father, and ye behold me no more;

11 Of judgement, because

the prince of this world hath been judged.

12 I have yet many things to say unto you, but ye cannot bear them now.

13 Howbeit when he, the Spirit of truth, is come, he shall guide you into all the truth: for he shall not speak from himself; but what things soever he shall hear, *these* shall he speak: and he shall declare unto you the things that are to come.

14 He shall glorify me: for he shall take of mine, and shall declare *it* unto you.

15 All things whatsoever the Father hath are mine: therefore said I, that he taketh of mine, and shall declare *it* unto you.

16 A little while, and ye behold me no more; and again a little while, and ye shall see me.

17 *Some* of his disciples therefore said one to another, What is this that he saith unto us, A little while, and ye behold me not; and again a little while, and ye

shall see me: and, Because I go to the Father?

18 They said therefore, What is this that he saith, A little while? We know not what he saith.

19 Jesus perceived that they were desirous to ask him, and he said unto them, Do ye inquire among yourselves concerning this, that I said, A little while, and ye behold me not, and again a little while, and ye shall see me?

20 Verily, verily, I say unto you, that ye shall weep and lament, but the world shall rejoice: ye shall be sorrowful, but your sorrow shall be turned into joy.

21 A woman when she is in travail hath sorrow, because her hour is come: but when she is delivered of the child, she remembereth no more the anguish, for the joy that a man is born into the world.

22 And ye therefore now have sorrow: but I will see you again, and your heart shall rejoice, and your joy no one taketh away from you.

23 And in that day ye shall ask me nothing. Verily, verily, I say unto you, If ye shall ask anything of the Father, he will give it you in my name.

24 Hitherto have ye asked nothing in my name: ask, and ye shall receive, that your joy may be fulfilled.

25 These things have I spoken unto you in proverbs: the hour cometh, when I shall no more speak unto you in proverbs, but shall tell you plainly of the Father.

26 In that day ye shall ask in my name: and I say not unto you, that I will pray the Father for you;

27 For the Father himself loveth you, because ye have loved me, and have believed that I came forth from the Father.

28 I came out from the Father, and am come into the world: again, I leave the

world, and go unto the Father.

29 His disciples say, Lo, now speakest thou plainly, and speakest no proverb.

30 Now know we that thou knowest all things, and needest not that any man should ask thee: by this we believe that thou camest forth from God.

31 Jesus answered them, Do ye now believe?

32 Behold, the hour cometh, yea, is come, that ye shall be scattered, every man to his own, and shall leave me alone: and *yet* I am not alone, because the Father is with me.

33 These things have I spoken unto you, that in me ye may have peace. In the world ye have tribulation: but be of good cheer; I have overcome the world.

## CHAPTER LVI.

THESE things spake Jesus; and lifting up his eyes to heaven, he said, Father, the hour is come; glorify thy Son, that the Son may glorify thee:

2 Even as thou gavest him authority over all flesh, that whatsoever thou hast given him, to them he should give eternal life.

3 And this is life eternal, that they should know thee the only true God, and him whom thou didst send, *even* Jesus Christ.

4 I glorified thee on the earth, having accomplished the work which thou hast given me to do.

5 And now, O Father, glorify thou me with thine own self with the glory which I had with thee before the world was.

6 I manifested thy name unto the men whom thou gavest me out of the world: thine they were, and thou gavest them to me; and they have kept thy word.

7 Now they know that all things whatsoever thou hast given me are from thee:

8 For the words which thou gavest me I have given

unto them; and they received *them*, and knew of a truth that I came forth from thee, and they believed that thou didst send me.

9 I pray for them: I pray not for the world, but for those whom thou hast given me; for they are thine:

10 And all things that are mine are thine, and thine are mine: and I am glorified in them.

11 And I am no more in the world, and these are in the world, and I come to thee. Holy Father, keep them in thy name which thou hast given me, that they may be one, even as we *are*.

12 While I was with them, I kept them in thy name which thou hast given me: and I guarded them, and not one of them perished, but the son of perdition; that the scripture might be fulfilled.

13 But now I come to thee; and these things I speak in the world, that they may have my joy fulfilled in themselves.

14 I have given them thy word; and the world hated them, because they are not of the world, even as I am not of the world.

15 I pray not that thou shouldest take them from the world, but that thou shouldest keep them from the evil *one*.

16 They are not of the world, even as I am not of the world.

17 Sanctify them in the truth: thy word is truth.

18 As thou didst send me into the world, even so sent I them into the world.

19 And for their sakes I sanctify myself, that they themselves also may be sanctified in truth.

20 Neither for these only do I pray, but for them also that believe on me through their word;

21 That they may all be one; even as thou, Father, *art* in me, and I in thee, that they also may be in us: that

JESUS AND HIS DISCIPLES GOING TO THE GARDEN OF GETHSEMANE.

the world may believe that thou didst send me.

22 And the glory which thou hast given me I have given unto them; that they may be one, even as we *are* one;

23 I in them, and thou in me, that they may be perfected into one; that the world may know that thou didst send me, and lovedst them, even as thou lovedst me.

24 Father, that which thou hast given me, I will that, where I am, they also may be with me; that they may behold my glory, which thou hast given me: for thou lovedst me before the foundation of the world.

25 O righteous Father, the world knew thee not, but I knew thee; and these knew that thou didst send me;

26 And I made known unto them thy name, and will make it known; that the love wherewith thou lovedst me may be in them, and I in them.

## CHAPTER LVII.

WHEN Jesus had spoken these words,

And when they had sung a hymn, he went forth with his disciples over the brook Kidron,

2 Then saith Jesus unto them, All ye shall be offended in me this night: for it is written, I will smite the shepherd, and the sheep of the flock shall be scattered abroad.

3 But after I am raised up, I will go before you into Galilee.

4 But Peter answered and said unto him, If all shall be offended in thee, I will never be offended.

### SATAN SIFTING PETER.

5 Jesus said unto him, Simon, Simon, behold, Satan asked to have you, that he might sift you as wheat:

6 But I made supplication for thee, that thy faith fail not: and do thou, when once thou hast turned again, stablish thy brethren.

7 And he said unto him, Lord, with thee I am ready to go both to prison and to death.

8 And Jesus saith unto him, Verily I say unto thee, that thou to-day, *even* this night, before the cock crow twice, shalt deny me thrice.

9 But he spake exceeding vehemently, If I must die with thee, I will not deny thee. And in like manner also said they all.

10 And he said unto them, When I sent you forth without purse, and wallet, and shoes, lacked ye anything?

11 And they said, Nothing. And he said unto them, But now, he that hath a purse, let him take it, and likewise a wallet: and he that hath none, let him sell his cloke, and buy a sword.

12 For I say unto you, that this which is written must be fulfilled in me, And he was reckoned with transgressors: for that which concerneth me hath fulfilment.

13 And they said, Lord, behold, here are two swords. And he said unto them, It is enough.

14 And they come unto a place which was named Gethsemane: a garden, into the which he entered, himself and his disciples.

15 Now Judas, also, which betrayed him, knew the place: for Jesus oft-times resorted thither with his disciples.

16 And he said unto them, Pray that ye enter not into temptation. Sit ye here, while I go yonder and pray.

### THE AGONY.

Friday morn early, April 7, A. D. 30.

17 And he took with him Peter and the two sons of Zebedee, and began to be sorrowful and sore troubled.

18 Then saith he unto them, My soul is exceeding sorrowful, even unto death: abide ye here, and watch with me.

19 And he went forward a little, and fell on his face, and prayed, saying, O my Father, if it be possible, let

THE PRAYER OF JESUS IN THE GARDEN.

this cup pass away from me; nevertheless, not as I will, but as thou wilt.

20 And when he rose up from his prayer, he came unto the disciples, and found them sleeping for sorrow.

21 And said unto them, Why sleep ye? rise and pray, that ye enter not into temptation.

22 And saith unto Peter, Simon, sleepest thou? couldest thou not watch with me one hour?

23 Watch and pray, that ye enter not into temptation: the spirit indeed is willing, but the flesh is weak.

24 Again, a second time he went away, and prayed, saying the same words. O my Father, if this cannot pass away, except I drink it, thy will be done.

25 And again he came, and found them sleeping, for their eyes were very heavy; and they wist not what to answer him. And he left them again, and went away, and prayed a third time.

26 And he said, Abba, Father, all things are possible unto thee; remove this cup from me: howbeit not what I will, but what thou wilt.

27 And there appeared unto him an angel from heaven, strengthening him.

28 And being in an agony he prayed more earnestly: and his sweat became as it were great drops of blood falling down upon the ground.

29 And he cometh the third time, and saith unto them, Sleep on now, and take your rest: it is enough; the hour is come; behold, the Son of man is betrayed into the hands of sinners.

30 Arise, let us be going: behold, he that betrayeth me is at hand.

31 And straightway, while he yet spake, cometh Judas, one of the twelve, and with him a multitude with swords and staves, from the chief priests and the scribes and the elders.

32 Now he that betrayed him had given them a token saying, Whomsoever I shall kiss, that is he; take him, and lead him away safely.

33 And straightway he came to Jesus, and said, Hail, Rabbi; and kissed him.

34 And Jesus said unto him,

Judas, betrayest thou the Son of man with a kiss?

35 Jesus therefore, knowing all the things that were coming upon him, went forth, and saith unto them, Whom seek ye?

36 They answered him, Jesus of Nazareth. Jesus saith unto them, I am *he*.

37 When therefore he said unto them, I am *he*, they went backward, and fell to the ground.

38 Again therefore he asked them, Whom seek ye? And they said, Jesus of Nazareth.

39 Jesus answered, I told you that I am *he*: if therefore ye seek me, let these go their way:

40 That the word might be fulfilled which he spake, Of those whom thou hast given me I lost not one.

41 Then they came and laid hands on Jesus, and took him.

42 And when they that were about him saw what would follow, they said, Lord, shall we smite with the sword?

43 Simon Peter therefore having a sword drew it, and struck the high priest's servant, and cut off his right ear. The servant's name was Malchus.

44 But Jesus answered and said, Suffer ye thus far. And he touched his ear, and healed him.

45 Jesus therefore said unto Peter, Put up the sword into the sheath; for all they that take the sword shall perish with the sword. The cup which the Father hath given me, shall I not drink it?

46 Or thinkest thou that I cannot beseech my Father,

THE KISS OF JUDAS.

and he shall even now send me more than twelve legions of angels?

47 How then should the scriptures be fulfilled, that thus it must be?

48 In that hour said Jesus to the multitudes, Are ye come out as against a robber with swords and staves to seize me?

49 When I was daily with you in the temple, ye stretched not forth your hands against me: but this is your hour, and the power of darkness.

50 Then all the disciples left him, and fled.

51 And a certain young man followed with him, having a linen cloth cast about him, over *his* naked *body*: and they lay hold on him;

52 but he left the linen cloth, and fled naked.

53 So the band and the chief captain, and the officers of the Jews, seized Jesus and bound him,

### TRIAL BEFORE ANNAS.

54 And led him to Annas first; for he was father in law to Caiaphas, which was high priest that year.

55 He, Annas, therefore asked Jesus of his disciples, and of his teaching.

56 Jesus answered him, I have spoken openly to the world; I ever taught in synagogues, and in the temple, where all the Jews come together; and in secret spake I nothing.

57 Why askest thou me? ask them that have heard *me*, what I spake unto them: behold, these know t h e things which I said.

58 And when he had said this, one of the officers standing by struck Jesus with his hand, saying, Answerest thou the high priest so?

59 Jesus answered him, If I have spoken evil, bear witness of the evil: but if well, why smitest thou me?

60· Annas therefore sent him bound unto Caiaphas the high priest.

61 And they led Jesus

away to the high priest: and there come together with him all the chief priests and the elders and the scribes.

## CHAPTER LVIII.

NOW Caiaphas was he which gave counsel to the Jews, that it was expedient that one man should die for the people.

2 And Simon Peter followed Jesus, and *so did* another disciple. Now that disciple was known unto the high priests, and entered in with Jesus into the court of the high priest.

3 But Peter was standing at the door without. So the other disciple, which was known unto the high priest, went out and spake unto her that kept the door, and brought in Peter.

4 Now the servants and the officers were standing *there*, having made a fire of coals;

5 For it was cold; and they were warming themselves: and Peter also was with them, standing and warming himself.

6 Now the chief priests and the whole council sought false witness against Jesus, that they might put him to death; and found it not.

7 And there stood up certain, and bare w i t n e s s against him, saying,

8 We heard him say, I will destroy this temple that is made with hands, and in three days I will build another made without hands.

9 And not even so did their witness agree together.

10 And the high priest stood up in the midst, and asked Jesus, saying, Answerest thou nothing? what is it which these witness against thee?

11 But he held his peace and answered nothing.

12 And the high priest said unto him, I adjure thee by the living God, that thou tell us whether thou be the Christ, the Son of God.

13 Art thou the Christ, the Son of the Blessed?

14 And Jesus said, I am: and ye shall see the Son of man sitting at the right hand of power, and coming with the clouds of heaven.

15 Then the high priest rent his garments, saying, He hath spoken blasphemy: what further need have we of witnesses? behold, now ye have heard the blasphemy:

16 What think ye? And they all condemned him to be worthy of death.

17 And some began to spit on him, and to cover his face, and to buffet him, and to say unto him, Prophesy: and the officers received him with blows of their hands.

18 And the men that held *Jesus* mocked him, and beat him.

19 And they blindfolded him, and asked him, saying, Prophesy: who is he that struck thee?

20 And many other things spake they against him, reviling him.

PETER'S REMORSE.

21 And as Peter was be-neath in the court, there cometh one of the maids of the high priest;

22 And seeing Peter warming himself, she looked upon him, and saith, Thou also wast with the Nazarene, *even* Jesus.

23 But he denied, saying, I neither know, nor under-stand what thou sayest: and he went out into the porch;

24 And when he was gone out into the porch, another *maid* saw him, and saith un-to them that were there, This man also was with Jesus the Nazarene.

25 But he again denied it.

26 And after a little while they that stood by came and said to Peter, Of a truth thou also art *one* of them; for thy speech betrayeth thee.

27 And one of the ser-vants of the high priest, be-ing a kinsman of him whose ear Peter cut off, saith, Did not I see thee in the garden with him?

28 Then began he to curse

and to swear, I know not the man. And straightway the cock crew.

29 And the Lord turned, and looked upon Peter.

30 And Peter remembered the word which Jesus had said, Before the cock crow, thou shalt deny me thrice.

31 And he went out, and wept bitterly.

## CHAPTER LIX.

### TRIAL BEFORE SANHEDRIN.

AND straightway in the morning as soon as it was day, the assembly of the elders of the people was gathered together, both chief priests and scribes; and they led him away into their council, saying,

2 If thou art the Christ, tell us. But he said unto them, If I tell you, ye will not believe:

3 And if I ask *you*, ye will not answer. But from henceforth shall the Son of man be seated at the right hand of the power of God.

4 And they all said, Art thou then the Son of God? And he said unto them, Ye say that I am.

5 And they said, What further need have we of witness? for we ourselves have heard from his own mouth.

6 And they bound him, and led him away, and delivered him up to Pilate the governor.

7 Then Judas, which betrayed him, when he saw that he was condemned, repented himself, and brought back the thirty pieces of silver to the chief priests and elders, saying,

8 I have sinned in that I betrayed innocent blood. But they said, What is that to us? see thou *to it*.

A. D. 30. Friday, April 7, at daybreak.

9 And he cast down the pieces of silver into the sanctuary, and departed; and he went away and hanged himself.

10 And the chief priests took the pieces of silver, and

PETER'S REPENTANCE.

said, It is not lawful to put them into the treasury, since it is the price of blood.

11 And they took counsel, and bought with them the potter's field, to bury strangers in.

12 Wherefore that field was called, T h e field o f blood, unto this day.

13 Then was fulfilled that which was spoken by Jeremiah the prophet, saying, And they took the thirty pieces of silver, the price of him that was priced, whom *certain* of the children of Israel did price;

14 And they gave them for the potter's field, as the Lord appointed me.

TRIALS BEFORE PILATE AND HEROD.

15 And now Jesus stood before the governor: and it was early;

16 The Jews themselves entered not into the palace, that they might not be defiled, but might eat the passover.

17 Pilate therefore went out unto them, and saith, What accusation bring ye against this man?

18 They answered a n d said unto him, If this man were not an evil-doer, we should not have delivered him up unto thee.

19 Pilate therefore said unto them, Take him yourselves, and judge him according to your law. The Jews said unto him, It is not lawful for us to put any man to death:

20 That the word of Jesus might be fulfilled, which he spake, signifying by what manner of death he should die.

21 And they began to accuse him, saying, We found this man perverting our nation, and forbidding to give tribute to Cæsar, and saying that he himself is Christ a king.

22. Pilate therefore entered again into the palace, and called Jesus, and said unto him, Art thou the King of the Jews?

23 Jesus answered, Sayest thou this of thyself, or did others tell it thee concerning me?

24 Pilate answered, Am I a Jew? Thine own nation and the chief priests delivered thee unto me: what hast thou done?

25 Jesus answered, My kingdom is not of this world: if my kingdom were of this world, then would my servants fight, that I should not be delivered to the Jews: but now is my kingdom not from hence.

26 Pilate therefore said unto him, Art thou a king, then? Jesus answered, Thou sayest that I am a king. To this end have I been born, and to this end am I come into the world, that I should bear witness unto the truth. Every one that is of the truth heareth my voice.

27 Pilate saith unto him, What is truth?

28 And when he had said this, he went out again unto the Jews, and saith unto them, I find no crime in him.

29 But they were the more urgent, saying, He stirreth up the people, teaching throughout all Judæa, and beginning from Galilee even unto this place.

30 But when Pilate heard it, he asked whether the man were a Galilæan.

31 And when he knew that he was of Herod's jurisdiction, he sent him unto Herod, who himself also was at Jerusalem in these days.

32 Now when Herod saw Jesus, he was exceeding glad: for he was of a long time desirous to see him, because he had heard concerning him; and he hoped to see some miracle done by him.

33 And he questioned him in many words; but he answered him nothing.

34 And the chief priests and the scribes stood, vehemently accusing him.

35 And Herod with his soldiers set him at nought,

CHRIST BEFORE PILATE.

and mocked him, and array-
ing him in gorgeous apparel
sent him back to Pilate.

36 And Herod and Pilate
became friends with each
other that very day: for before they were at enmity between themselves.

37 And while Pilate was
sitting on the judgement-
seat, his wife sent unto him,
saying, Have thou nothing to
do with that righteous man:
for I have suffered many
things this day in a dream
because of him.

38 And Pilate called to-
gether the chief priests and
the rulers and the people,

39 And said unto them,
Ye brought unto me this
man, as one that perverteth
the people: and behold, I,
having examined him before
you, found no fault in this
man touching those things
whereof ye accuse him:

40 No, nor yet Herod: for
he sent him back unto us;
and behold, nothing worthy
of death hath been done by
him.

41 I will therefore chastise
him, and release him.

42 Now at a feast the governor was wont to release
unto the multitude one prisoner, whom they would.

43 And they had then a
notable prisoner, called Barabbas, *lying* bound with
them that had made insur-
rection, men who in the
insurrection had committed
murder.

44 And the multitude
went up and began to ask
him *to do* as he was wont to
do unto them.

45 When therefore they
were gathered together, Pilate said unto them, Whom
will ye that I release unto you? Barabbas, or Jesus
which is called Christ the
King of the Jews?

46 For he perceived that
for envy the chief priests had
delivered him up.

47 But the chief priests
and the elders persuaded the
multitudes that they should
ask for Barabbas, and de-
stroy Jesus.

48 And they cried out all together, saying, Away with this man, and release unto us Barabbas:

49 And Pilate spake unto them again, desiring to release Jesus;

50 They cried out therefore again saying, Not this man, but Barabbas. Now Barabbas was a robber.

51 And Pilate again answered and said unto them, What then shall I do unto Jesus which is called Christ? They all say, Let him be crucified.

52 And he said, Why, what evil hath he done? But they cried out exceedingly, saying, Crucify *him*, crucify *him*.

53 He said unto them, I have found no cause of death in him: I w i l l therefore chastise him and release him.

54 And the soldiers led him away within the court, which is the Prætorium; and they call together the whole band.

55 And they clothe him with purple, and plaiting a crown of thorns, they put it on him; and they began to salute him, Hail, King of the Jews!

56 And they smote his head with a reed, and did spit upon him, and bowing their knees worshipped him.

57 And Pilate went out again, and saith unto them, Behold, I bring him out to you, that ye may know that I find no crime in him.

58 Jesus therefore came out, wearing the crown of thorns and the purple garment. And *Pilate* saith unto them, Behold, the man!

59 When therefore t h e chief priests and the officers saw him, they cried out, saying, Crucify *him*, crucify *him*.

60 Pilate saith unto them, Take him yourselves, and crucify him: for I find no crime in him.

61 The J e w s answered him, We have a law, and by that law he ought to die, be-

"BEHOLD THE MAN."

cause he made himself the Son of God.

62 When Pilate therefore heard this saying, he was the more afraid;

63 And he entered into the palace again, and saith unto Jesus, Whence art thou? But Jesus gave him no answer.

64 Pilate therefore saith unto him, Speakest thou not unto me? knowest thou not that I have power to release thee, and have power to crucify thee?

65 Jesus answered him, Thou wouldest have no power against me, except it were given thee from above: therefore he that delivered me unto thee hath greater sin.

66 Upon this Pilate sought to release him: but the Jews cried out, saying, If thou release this man, thou art not Cæsar's friend: every one that maketh himself a king speaketh against Cæsar.

67 When Pilate therefore heard these words, he brought Jesus out, and sat down on the judgement-seat at a place called The Pavement, but in Hebrew, Gabbatha.

68 Now it was the Preparation of the passover: it was about the sixth hour. And he saith unto the Jews, Behold, your King!

69 They therefore cried out, Away with *him*, away with *him*, crucify him. Pilate saith unto them, Shall I crucify your King?

70 The chief priests answered, We have no king but Cæsar.

71 So when Pilate saw that he prevailed nothing, but rather that tumult was arising, he took water, and washed his hands before the multitude, saying, I am innocent of the blood of this righteous man: see ye *to it*.

72 And all the people answered and said, His blood *be* on us, and on our children; and their voices prevailed.

73 Then Pilate, wishing

to content the multitude, released him that for insurrection and murder had been cast into prison, whom they asked for; but Jesus he delivered up to their will.

74 And when they had mocked him, they took off from him the purple, and put on him his garments. And they lead him out to crucify him.

## CHAPTER LX.

### THE CRUCIFIXION.

A. D. 30, April 7, 9 A.M.

JESUS therefore went out, bearing the cross.

2 And they compel one passing by, Simon of Cyrene, coming from the country, the father of Alexander and Rufus, to go *with them*, and to bear the cross, after Jesus.

3 And there followed him a great multitude of the people, and of women who bewailed and lamented him.

4 But Jesus turning unto them said, Daughters of Jerusalem, weep not for me, but weep for yourselves, and for your children.

5 For behold, the days are coming, in which they shall say, Blessed are the barren, and the wombs that never bare, and the breasts that never gave suck.

6 Then shall they begin to say to the mountains, Fall on us; and to the hills, Cover us.

7 For if they do these things in the green tree, what shall be done in the dry?

8 And there were also two others, malefactors, led with him to be put to death.

9 And when they were come unto a place called Golgotha, that is to say, The place of a skull, they gave him wine to drink mingled with gall: and when he had tasted it, he would not drink.

10 There they crucified him, and the malefactors, one on the right hand and the other on the left, and Jesus in the midst.

11 And Jesus said, Father,

"Daughters of Jerusalem Weep Not for Me"

forgive them; for they know not what they do.

12 The soldiers, when they had crucified Jesus, took his garments, and made four parts, to every soldier a part; and also the coat: now the coat was without seam, woven from the top throughout.

13 They said therefore one to another, Let us not rend it, but cast lots for it, whose it shall be: that the scripture might be fulfilled, which saith,

They parted my garments among them,

And upon my vesture did they cast lots.

These things therefore the soldiers did.

14 It was the third hour, and they sat and watched him there.

15 And Pilate wrote a title also, and put it on the cross. And there was written, JESUS OF NAZARETH, THE KING OF THE JEWS.

16 This title therefore read many of the Jews: for the place where Jesus was crucified was nigh to the city: and it was written in Hebrew, *and* in Latin, *and* in Greek.

17 The chief priests of the Jews therefore said to Pilate, Write not, The king of the Jews; but, that he said, I am king of the Jews.

18 Pilate answered, What I have written I have written.

19 And the people stood beholding. And the rulers also scoffed at him, saying, He saved others; let him save himself, if this is the Christ of God, his chosen.

20 And the soldiers also mocked him, coming to him, offering him vinegar, and saying,

21 If thou art the King of the Jews, save thyself.

22 And they that passed by railed on him, wagging their heads, and saying,

23 Thou that destroyest the temple, and buildest it in three days, save thyself: if thou art the Son of God, come down from the cross.

24 In like manner also the chief priests mocking *him*, with the scribes and elders, said, He saved others;

25 Himself he cannot save. He is the King of Israel; let him now come down from the cross, and we will believe on him.

26 He trusteth on God; let him deliver him now, if he desireth him: for he said, I am the Son of God.

27 And one of the malefactors which were hanged railed on him, saying, Art not thou the Christ? save thyself and us.

28 But the other answered, and rebuking him said, Dost thou not even fear God, seeing thou art in the same condemnation?

29 And we indeed justly; for we receive the due reward of our deeds: but this man hath d o n e nothing amiss.

30 And he said, Jesus, remember me when thou comest in thy kingdom.

31 And he said unto him, Verily I say unto thee, To-day shalt thou be with me in Paradise.

32 There were standing by the cross of Jesus his mother, and his mother's sister, Mary the *wife* of Clopas, and Mary Magdalene.

33 When Jesus therefore saw his mother, and the disciple standing by, whom he loved, he saith unto his mother, Woman, behold, thy son!

34 Then saith he to the disciple, Behold, thy mother! And from that hour the disciple took her unto his own *home*.

35 And when the sixth hour was come, there was darkness over the whole land until the ninth hour.

36 And at the ninth hour Jesus cried with a loud voice, Eloi, Eloi, lama sabachthani? which is, being interpreted, My God, my God, why hast thou forsaken me?

37 And some of them that stood by, when they heard

"Woman, Behold thy Son."

it, said, Behold, he calleth Elijah.

38 After this, Jesus, knowing that all things are now finished, that the scripture might be accomplished, saith, I thirst.

39 There was set there a vessel full of vinegar:

40 And one ran, and filling a sponge full of vinegar, put it on a reed, and gave him to drink, saying, Let be; let us see whether Elijah cometh to take him down.

41 When Jesus therefore had received the vinegar, he said, It is finished:

42 And when he had cried with a loud voice, he said, Father, into thy hands I commend my spirit: and having said this, he gave up the ghost.

43 And behold, the veil of the temple was rent in twain from the top to the bottom; and the earth did quake; and the rocks were rent:

44 And the tombs were opened; and many bodies of the saints that had fallen asleep were raised;

45 And coming forth out of the tombs after his resurrection they entered into the holy city and appeared unto many.

46 Now the centurion, and they that were with him watching Jesus, when they saw the earthquake, and the things that were done, feared exceedingly, saying, Truly this was the Son of God.

47 And the centurion glorified God, saying, Certainly this was a righteous man.

48 And all the multitudes that came together to this sight, when they beheld the things that were done, returned smiting their breasts.

49 And there were also women beholding from afar: among whom *were* both Mary Magdalene, and Mary the mother of James the less and of Joses, and Salome;

50 Who, when he was in Galilee, followed him, and ministered unto him; and many other women which came up with him unto Jerusalem.

51 The Jews therefore, because it was the Preparation, that the bodies should not remain on the cross upon the sabbath (for the day of that sabbath was a high *day*), asked of Pilate that their legs might be broken, and *that* they might be taken away.

52 The soldiers therefore came, and brake the legs of the first, and of the other which was crucified with him:

53 But when they came to Jesus, and saw that he was dead already, they brake not his legs:

54 Howbeit one of the soldiers with a spear pierced his side, and straightway there came out blood and water.

55 And he that hath seen hath borne witness, and his witness is true: and he knoweth that he saith true, that ye also may believe.

56 For these things came to pass, that the scripture might be fulfilled, A bone of him shall not be broken.

57 And again another scripture saith, They shall look on him whom they pierced.

CHAPTER LXI.

AND behold, a man named Joseph, who was a councillor, a good man and a righteous

2 (He had not consented to their counsel and deed), *a man* of Arimathæa, a city of the Jews, who was looking for the kingdom of God:

3 This man when even was come, being a disciple of Jesus, but secretly for fear of the Jews, asked of Pilate that he might take away the body of Jesus:

4 And Pilate marvelled if he were already dead: and calling unto him the centurion, he asked him whether he had been any while dead.

5 And when he learned it of the centurion, he granted the corpse to Joseph.

6 And he bought a linen cloth, and taking him down, wound him in the linen cloth.

THE MOTHER'S SORROW.

7 And there came also Nicodemus, he who at the first came to him by night, bringing a mixture of myrrh and aloes, about a hundred pound *weight*.

8 So they took the body of Jesus, and bound it in linen cloths with the spices, as the custom of the Jews is to bury.

9 Now in the place where he was crucified there was a garden; and in the garden a new tomb wherein was never man yet laid. Joseph's own new tomb, which he had hewn out in the rock:

10 There then because of the Jews' Preparation (for the tomb was nigh at hand) they laid Jesus.

11 And he rolled a great stone to the door of the tomb, and departed.

12 And the women, which had come with him out of Galilee, followed after, and beheld the tomb, and how his body was laid.

13 And Mary Magdalene was there, and the other Mary, sitting over against the sepulchre. And they returned, and prepared spices and ointments.

And on the sabbath they rested according to the commandment.

### THE RESURRECTION.

14 Now on the morrow, which is *the day* after the Preparation, the chief priests and the Pharisees were gathered together unto Pilate, saying,

15 Sir, we remember that that deceiver said, while he was yet alive, After three days I rise again.

16 Command therefore that the sepulchre be made sure until the third day, lest haply his disciples come and steal him away, and say unto the people, He is risen from the dead: and the last error will be worse than the first.

17 Pilate said unto them, Ye have a guard: go your way, make it *as* sure as ye can.

18 So they went, and made the sepulchre sure, sealing the stone, the guard being with them.

19 And as it began to dawn toward the first *day* of the week, behold, there was a great earthquake; for an angel of the Lord descended from heaven, and came and rolled away the stone, and sat upon it.

20 His appearance was as lightning, and his raiment white as snow:

21 And for fear of him the watchers did quake, and became as dead men.

22 And when the sabbath was past, Mary Magdalene, and Mary the *mother* of James, and Salome, bought spices, that they might come and anoint him.

23 And very early on the first day of the week, they come to the tomb when the sun was risen.

24 And they were saying among themselves, W h o shall roll us away the stone from the door of the tomb?

25 And looking up, they see that the stone is rolled back: for it was exceeding great.

26 Mary Magdalene runneth therefore, and cometh to Simon Peter, and to the other disciple, whom Jesus loved, and saith unto them, They have taken away the Lord out of the tomb, and we know not where they have laid him.

27 But the other women entering into the tomb, they saw a young man sitting on the right side, arrayed in a white robe; and they were amazed.

28 And h e saith unto them, Be not amazed: ye seek Jesus, the Nazarene, which hath been crucified, even as he said; he is risen. He is not here: behold, the place where they laid him!

29 And go quickly, and tell his disciples, and Peter. He is risen from the dead; and lo, he goeth before you into Galilee; lo, I have told you.

30 And they went out, and fled from the tomb; for trembling and astonishment had come upon them:

THE WOMEN AT THE TOMB.

31 And it came to pass, while they were perplexed thereabout, behold, two men stood by them in dazzling apparel:

32 And as they were affrighted, and bowed down their faces to the earth, they said unto them, Why seek ye the living among the dead?

33 He is not here, but is risen: remember how he spake unto you when he was yet in Galilee,

34 Saying that the Son of man must be delivered up into the hands of sinful men, and be crucified, and the third day rise again.

35 And they remembered his words, and returned from the tomb, with fear and great joy, and ran to bring his disciples word. And they said nothing to any one; for they were afraid.

36 Now while they were going, behold, some of the guard came into the city, and told the chief priests all the things that were come to pass.

37 And when they were assembled with the elders, and had taken counsel, they gave large money unto the soldiers,

38 Saying, Say ye, His disciples came by night, and stole him away while we slept.

39 And if this come to the governor's ears, we will persuade him, and rid you of care.

40 So they took the money, and did as they were taught: and this saying was spread abroad among the Jews, *and continueth* until this day.

## CHAPTER LXII.

MARY Magdalene cometh to Simon Peter, and to the other disciple, whom Jesus loved, and saith unto them, They have taken away the Lord out of the tomb, and we know not where they have laid him.

2 Peter therefore went forth, and the other disciple, and they went toward the tomb.

3 And they ran both together: and the other disciple outran Peter, and came first to the tomb;

4 And stooping and looking in, he seeth the linen cloths lying; yet entered he not in.

5 Simon Peter therefore also cometh, following him, and entered into the tomb; and he beholdeth the linen cloths lying,

6 And the napkin, that was upon his head, not lying with the linen cloths, but rolled up in a place by itself.

7 Then entered in therefore the other disciple also, which came first to the tomb, and he saw, and believed.

8 For as yet they knew not the scripture, that he must rise again from the dead.

9 So the disciples went away again unto their own home, wondering at that which was come to pass.

10 But Mary was standing without at the tomb weeping: so, as she wept, she stooped and looked into the tomb,

11 And she beholdeth two angels in white sitting, one at the head, and one at the feet, where the body of Jesus had lain.

12 And they say unto her, Woman, why weepest thou? She saith unto them, Because they have taken away my Lord, and I know not where they have laid him.

13 When she had thus said, she turned herself back, and beholdeth Jesus standing, and knew not that it was Jesus.

14 Jesus saith unto her, Woman, why weepest thou? whom seekest thou. She, supposing him to be the gardener, saith unto him, Sir, if thou hast borne him hence, tell me where thou hast laid him, and I will take him away.

15 Jesus saith unto her, Mary. She turneth herself, and saith unto him in Hebrew, Rabboni; which is to say, Master.

" Rabboni, Master."

16 Jesus saith to her, Touch me not; for I am not yet ascended unto the Father: but go unto my brethren, and say to them, I ascend unto my Father and your Father, and my God and your God.

17 Mary Magdalene cometh and telleth the disciples, I have seen the Lord; and *how that* he had said these things unto her.

## CHAPTER LXIII.

NOW when he was risen early on the first day of the week, he appeared first to Mary Magdalene, from whom he had cast out seven devils.

2 She went and told them that had been with him, as they mourned and wept.

3 And they, when they heard that he was alive, and had been seen of her, disbelieved.

4 And as Joanna, and Mary the *mother* of James: and the other women with them departed quickly from the tomb with fear and great joy, and ran to bring his disciples word,

5 Behold, Jesus met them, saying, All hail. And they came and took hold of his feet, and worshipped him.

6 Then saith Jesus unto them, Fear not: go tell my brethren that they depart into Galilee, and there shall they see me.

7 Joanna, and Mary the *mother* of James: and the other women with them told these things unto the apostles.

8 And these words appeared in their sight as idle talk; and they disbelieved them.

9 And after these things he was manifested in another form unto two of them, as they walked, on their way into the country, to a village named Emmaus, which was threescore furlongs from Jerusalem.

10 And they communed with each other of all these things which had happened.

Sunday afternoon, April 9, A. D. 30.

11 And it came to pass, while they communed and questioned together, that Jesus himself drew near, and went with them.

12 But their eyes were holden that they should not know him.

13 And he said unto them, What communications are these that ye have one with another, as ye walk? And they stood still, looking sad.

14 And one of them, named Cleopas, answering said unto him, Dost thou alone sojourn in Jerusalem and not know the things which are come to pass there in these days?

15 And he said unto them, What things? And they said unto him, The things concerning Jesus of Nazareth, which was a prophet mighty in deed and word before God and all the people:

16 And how the chief priests and our rulers delivered him up to be condemned to death, and crucified him.

17 But we hoped that it was he which should redeem Israel. Yea and beside all this, it is now the third day since these things came to pass.

18 Moreover certain women of our company amazed us, having been early at the tomb;

19 And when they found not his body, they came, saying, that they had also seen a vision of angels, which said that he was alive.

20 And certain of them that were with us went to the tomb, and found it even so as the women had said: but him they saw not.

21 And he said unto them, O foolish men, and slow of heart to believe in all that the prophets have spoken!

22 Behoved it not the Christ to suffer these things, and to enter into his glory?

23 And beginning from Moses and from all the prophets, he interpreted to them

THE SUPPER AT EMMAUS.

in all the scriptures the things concerning himself.

24 And they drew nigh unto the village, whither they were going: and he made as though he would go further.

25 And they constrained him, saying, Abide with us: for it is toward evening, and the day is now far spent. And he went in to abide with them.

26 And it came to pass, when he had sat down with them to meat, he took the bread, and blessed it, and brake, and gave to them.

27 And their eyes were opened, and they knew him; and he vanished out of their sight.

28 And they said one to another, Was not our heart burning within us, while he spake to us in the way, while he opened to us the scriptures?

29 And they rose up that very hour, and returned to Jerusalem, and found the eleven gathered together, and them that were with them, saying, The Lord is risen indeed, and hath appeared to Simon.

30 And they rehearsed the things *that happened* in the way, and how he was known of them in the breaking of the bread.

Sunday evening, April 9, A. D. 30.

31 And as they spake these things, and when the doors were shut where the disciples were, for fear of the Jews, Jesus himself stood in the midst, and said unto them, Peace *be* unto you.

32 But they were terrified and affrighted, and supposed that they beheld a spirit.

33 And he said unto them, Why are ye troubled? and wherefore do reasonings arise in your heart?

34 See my hands and my feet, that it is I myself: handle me, and see; for a spirit hath not flesh and bones, as ye behold me having.

35 And when he had said this, he shewed them his hands and his feet.

36 And while they still disbelieved for joy, and wondered, he said unto them, Have ye here anything to eat?

37 And they gave him a piece of a broiled fish. And he took it, and did eat before them.

38 And he u p b r a i d e d them with their unbelief and hardness of heart, because they believed n o t them which had seen him after he was risen.

39 And he said unto them, These are my words which I spake unto you, while I was yet with you, how that all things must needs be fulfilled, which are written in the law of Moses, and the prophets, and the psalms, concerning me.

40 Then opened he their mind, that they might understand the scriptures;

41 And he said unto them, Thus it is written, that the Christ should suffer, and rise again from the dead the third day;

42 And that repentance and remission of sins should be preached in his name unto all the nations, beginning from Jerusalem.

43 Ye are witnesses of these things.

44 And he said unto them, Go ye into all the world, and preach the gospel to the whole creation.

45 He that believeth and is baptized shall be saved; but he that disbelieveth shall be condemned.

46 And these signs shall follow them that believe: in my name shall they cast out devils; they shall speak with new tongues;

47 They shall take up serpents, and if they drink any deadly thing, it shall in no wise hurt them; they shall lay hands on the sick, and they shall recover.

48 Then Jesus said to them again, Peace *be* unto you: as the Father hath sent me, even so send I you.

49 And when he had said this, he breathed on them,

"My Lord and My God."

and saith unto them, Receive ye the Holy Ghost:

50 Whose soever sins ye forgive, they are forgiven unto them; whose soever *sins* ye retain, they are retained.

51 But Thomas, one of the twelve, called Didymus, was not with them when Jesus came.

52 The other disciples therefore said unto him, We have seen the Lord. But he said unto them, Except I shall see in his hands the print of the nails, and put my finger into the print of the nails, and put my hand into his side, I will not believe.

Sunday evening, April 16, A. D. 30.

53 And after eight days again his disciples were within, and Thomas with them. Jesus cometh, the doors being shut, and stood in the midst, and said, Peace *be* unto you.

54 Then saith he to Thomas, Reach hither thy finger, and see my hands; and reach *hither* thy hand, and put it into my side: and be not faithless, but believing.

55 Thomas answered and said unto him, My Lord and my God.

56 Jesus saith unto him, Because thou hast seen me, thou hast believed: blessed *are* they that have not seen, and *yet* have believed.

## CHAPTER LXIV.

April or May, A.D. 30.

AFTER these things Jesus manifested himself again to the disciples at the sea of Tiberias; and he manifested *himself* on this wise.

2 There were together Simon Peter, and Thomas called Didymus, and Nathanael of Cana in Galilee, and the *sons* of Zebedee, and two other of his disciples.

3 Simon Peter saith unto them, I go a fishing. They say unto him, We also come with thee. They went forth, and entered into the boat;

and that night they took nothing.

4 But when day was now breaking, Jesus stood on the beach: howbeit the disciples knew not that it was Jesus.

5 Jesus therefore saith unto them, Children, have ye aught to eat? They answered him, No.

6 And he said unto them, Cast the net on the right side of the boat, and ye shall find. They cast therefore, and now they were not able to draw it for the multitude of fishes.

7 That disciple therefore whom Jesus loved saith unto Peter, It is the Lord. So when Simon Peter heard that it was the Lord, he girt his coat about him (for he was naked), and cast himself into the sea.

8 But the other disciples came in the little boat (for they were not far from the land, but about two hundred cubits off), dragging the net *full* of fishes.

9 So when they got out upon the land, they see a fire of coals there, and fish laid thereon, and bread.

10 Jesus saith unto them, Bring of the fish which ye have now taken.

11 Simon Peter therefore went up, and drew the net to land, full of great fishes, a hundred and fifty and three: and for all there were so many, the net was not rent.

12 Jesus saith unto them, Come *and* break your fast. And none of the disciples durst inquire of him, Who art thou? knowing that it was the Lord.

13 Jesus cometh, and taketh the bread, and giveth them, and the fish likewise.

14 This is now the third time that Jesus was manifested to the disciples, after that he was risen from the dead.

15 So when they had broken their fast, Jesus saith to Simon Peter, Simon, *son* of John, lovest thou me more than these? He saith unto him, Yea, Lord; thou

"Children, Have Ye Any Meat?"

knowest that I love thee. He saith unto him, Feed my lambs.

16 He saith to him again a second time, Simon, *son* of John, lovest thou me? He saith unto him, Yea, Lord; thou knowest that I love thee. He saith unto him, Tend my sheep.

17 He saith unto him the third time, Simon, *son* of John, lovest thou me?

18 Peter was grieved because he said unto him the third time, Lovest thou me? And he said unto him, Lord, thou knowest all things; thou knowest that I love thee.

19 Jesus said unto him, Feed my sheep.

20 Verily, verily, I say unto thee, When thou wast young, thou girdedst thyself, and walkedst whither thou wouldest: but when thou shalt be old, thou shalt stretch forth thy hands, and another shall gird thee, and carry thee whither thou wouldest not.

21 Now this he spake, signifying by what manner of death he should glorify God. And when he had spoken this, he saith unto him, Follow me.

22 Peter, turning about, seeth the disciple whom Jesus loved following; which also leaned back on his breast at the supper, and said, Lord, who is he that betrayeth thee?

23 Peter therefore seeing him saith to Jesus, Lord, and what shall this man do?

24 Jesus saith unto him, If I will that he tarry till I come, what *is that* to thee? follow thou me.

25 This saying therefore went forth among the brethren, that that disciple should not die: yet Jesus said not unto him, that he should not die; but, If I will that he tarry till I come, what *is that* to thee?

26 This is the disciple which beareth witness of these things, and wrote these things: and we know that his witness is true.

## CHAPTER LXV.

THEN the eleven disciples went into Galilee, unto the mountain where Jesus had appointed them.

2 And he appeared to above five hundred brethren at once, of whom the greater part remain until now, but some are fallen asleep:

3 And when they saw him, they worshipped *him*: but some doubted.

4 And Jesus came to them and spake unto them, saying, All authority, hath been given unto me in heaven and on earth.

5 Go ye therefore, and make disciples of all the nations, baptizing them into the name of the Father and of the Son and of the Holy Ghost:

6 Teaching them to observe all things whatsoever I commanded you: and lo, I am with you alway, even unto the end of the world.

7 Afterward he appeared to James; then to all the apostles; to whom he also shewed himself alive after his passion by many proofs, appearing unto them by the space of forty days, and speaking the things concerning the kingdom of God:

8 And, being assembled together with them, he charged them not to depart from Jerusalem, but to wait for the promise of the Father, which, *said he*, ye heard from me:

9 For John indeed baptized with water; but ye shall be baptized with the Holy Ghost not many days hence.

10 They therefore, when they were come together, asked him, saying, Lord, dost thou at this time restore the kingdom to Israel?

11 And he said unto them, It is not for you to know times or seasons, which the Father hath set within his own authority.

12 But ye shall receive power, when the Holy Ghost

THE ASCENSION.

is come upon you: and ye shall be my witnesses both in Jerusalem, and in all Judæa and Samaria, and unto the uttermost parts of the earth.

13 And behold, I send forth the promise of my Father upon you: but tarry ye in the city, until ye be clothed with power from on high.

### THE ASCENSION.

May 18, A. D. 30.

14 And he led them out until *they were* over against Bethany: and he lifted up his hands, and blessed them.

15 And it came to pass, while he blessed them, he parted from them, and was carried up into heaven. And a cloud received him out of their sight.

16 And while they were looking stedfastly into heaven as he went, behold, two men stood by them in white apparel; which also said,

17 Ye men of Galilee, why stand ye looking into heaven? this Jesus, which was received up from you into heaven, shall so come in like manner as ye beheld him going into heaven.

18 And they worshipped him, and returned to Jerusalem with great joy:

19 And were continually in the temple, blessing God.

20 And the word of God increased, and the number of the disciples multiplied in Jerusalem exceedingly; and a great company of the priests were obedient to the faith.

21 And they went forth, and preached everywhere, the Lord working with them, and confirming the word by the signs that followed.

The twelfth appearance of our Lord after the resurrec-rection was made after His ascension.

We cite the words of the Evangelist Luke in reference to that ever memorable and glorious event.

### ACTS OF THE APOSTLES, CHAP. VII., VERSES 55, 56, 59, 60.

1 Stephen, being full of the Holy Ghost, looked up stedfastly into heaven, and saw the glory of God, and Jesus standing on the right hand of God,

2 And said, Behold I see the heavens opened, and the Son of man standing on the right hand of God.

3 And they stoned Stephen, calling upon *the Lord*, and saying, Lord Jesus, receive my spirit.

4 And he kneeled down and cried with a loud voice, Lord, lay not this sin to their charge.

And when he had said this, he fell asleep.

# INDEX.

| CHAP. P. | EVENTS. | PLACE. | MATT. | MARK. | LUKE. | JOHN. |
|---|---|---|---|---|---|---|
| XI..74. | The Palsied Cured | Capernaum | ..... | 2: 1, 2. | 5: 17-19. | ..... |
| | | | ..... | 2: 5-11. | 5: 25, 26. | ..... |
| | | | ..... | 3: 7. | 5: 1-11. | ..... |
| XI..77. | The Draught of Fishes. | Gennesaret. | | | | |
| XI..78. | The Call of Matthew. | Near Capernaum | 9: 9-11. | 2: 14. | 5: 27-32. | |
| | | | 9: 13-15. | 2: 21. | 5: 36. | |
| | | | 9: 17. | | 5: 39. | 5: 1-47. |
| XII..81. | The Pool of Bethesda. | Jerusalem | 12: 2, 5-7. | 2: 26-28. | 6: 1, 3, 4. | |
| XIII..89. | The Sabbath Made for Man. | | 12: 10-13. | 3: 5-12. | 6: 6-9. | |
| XIII..89. | The Withered Hand. | Capernaum | 12: 15, 17-21. | | 6: 11. | |
| | | | 10: 2-4. | 3: 14, 15. | 6: 12-16. | |
| XIV..93. | All Night in Prayer. | Horns of Hattin | | 3: 17, 19. | 6: 17-19. | |
| XIV..94. | The Sermon on the Mount. | " " " | 5: 1-48. | | 6: 23-28. | |
| | | | | | 6: 30-31. | |
| | | | | | 6: 34-36. | |
| XV..102. | The Sermon on the Mount. | " " " | 6: 1-34. | | 6: 45, 46. | |
| | | | | | 7: 1-9. | |
| XVI..109. | The Sermon on the Mount. | " " " | 7: 1-29. | | 7: 1-27. | |
| XVII..113. | The Centurion's Faith. | Capernaum | 8: 6, 7, 11-13. | | 7: 29-35. | |
| XVII..114. | The Widow's Son. | Nain | 11: 11-15. | | 7: 36-50. | |
| | | | 11: 20-30. | | 8: 1-3. | |
| XVIII..122. | The Woman a Sinner. | Galilee | 12: 22-24. | 3: 20, 21. | 11: 17-23. | |
| XVIII..125. | Blasphemy. | | 12: 32-37. | 3: 28-30. | | |
| XVIII..125. | Healing of a Demoniac. | Capernaum | | | | |
| XVIII..129. | The Pharisees Denounced. | By the Sea of Galilee | 12: 38-50. | | 8: 16, 19. | |
| | | | 6: 22, 23. | | 11: 35, 36. | |
| | | | | | 8: 21. | |
| XIX..130. | The Pharisees Denounced. | ..... | | | 11: 37-12: 9. | |
| | | | | | 12: 11-13: 9. | |

| CHAP. P. | EVENTS. | PLACE. | MATT. | MARK. | LUKE. | JOHN. |
|---|---|---|---|---|---|---|
| XX..145. | The Parables | By the Sea of Galilee | 13: 1-17. | 4: 26-29. | 8: 11-15. | ...... |
| | | | 13: 23-52. | 4: 10, 14. | 8: 18. | ...... |
| XXI..154. | | | ...... | 4: 21, 22. | 9: 57-62. | ...... |
| XXI..154. | The Tempest Stilled | On the Sea of Galilee | ...... | 4: 35-41. | ...... | ...... |
| XXI..157. | Demons Enter into Swine | Gergesa | 8: 32, 34. | 5: 1-8. | 8: 29-31. | ...... |
| | | | | 5: 11-13. | 8: 34, 35. | ...... |
| | | | | 5: 16, 18-21. | 8: 37, 40. | ...... |
| XXII..161. | Jairus' Daughter | Capernaum | 9: 19. | 5: 22, 23. | 8: 42. | ...... |
| XXII..161. | The Issue of Blood | " | 9: 20-24. | 5: 26, 27. | 8: 44. | ...... |
| | | | 9: 26. | 5: 29-31. | 8: 46-51. | ...... |
| | | | | 5: 34-36. | 8: 53. | ...... |
| | | | | 5: 39, 41, 42. | 8: 55, 56. | ...... |
| XXII..165. | The Blind See and the Dumb Speak | Capernaum | 9: 27-34. | | | ...... |
| XXIII..165. | The Twelve Sent Out | Galilee | 9: 35-38. | 6: 7, 11. | 9: 2, 6. | ...... |
| XXIII..166. | | | 10: 1, 11: 1. | 6: 13, 14. | | ...... |
| | | | 10: 5-13. | 6: 15. | | ...... |
| | | | 10: 15-42. | | | ...... |
| XXIII..173. | The Baptist Beheaded | Castle Macherus | 14: 1, 5, 12. | 6: 16-29. | | ...... |
| XXIV..174. | The Five Thousand Fed | Near Bethsaida | 14: 14, 21. | 6: 30-34. | 9: 11, 12. | 6: 1, 2. |
| | | | 14: 23, 24. | 6: 37, 38. | | 6: 5-10, 12. |
| | | | | 6: 40-43. | | 6: 14, 15. |
| | | | | 6: 45. | | 6: 18. |
| XXIV..178. | Jesus Walks on the Sea | Sea of Galilee | 14: 28-33. | 6: 48-56. | | 6: 21. |
| XXIV..181. | The Bread of Life | Capernaum | | | | 6: 22-27. |
| XXV..182. | The Bread of Life | " | | | | 6: 28-71. |
| XXVI..189. | The Traditions of Men | | 15: 3, 12-16. | 7: 1-13. | | ...... |
| | | | 15: 18, 20. | 7: 15, 17-19. | | ...... |
| | | | | 7: 21, 22. | | ...... |
| XXVI..193. | The Syrophœnician Woman | Region of Tyre and Sidon | 15: 22-25. | 7: 24-30. | | ...... |
| | | | 15: 28. | | | ...... |

| CHAP. P. | EVENTS. | PLACE. | MATT. | MARK. | LUKE. | JOHN. |
|---|---|---|---|---|---|---|
| XXVII..194. | Speech Given | Decapolis | 15: 29. | 7: 31-37. | | |
| XXVII..197. | The Lame and Blind and Maimed | " | 15: 30, 31. | 8: 1-15. | | |
| XXVII..197. | Four Thousand Fed | " | 15: 38, 39. 16: 2-4, 7-9. 16: 11, 12. | 8: 17-21. | | |
| XXVIII..201. | Blind Man Healed | Bethsaida | | 8: 22-27. | | |
| XXVIII..201. | Who Say Ye that I Am? | | 16: 13, 14. 16: 16-20. | | 9: 18-20. | |
| XXVIII..202. | Jesus Predicts His Death | Casarea Philippi | 16: 21-23. 16: 26-28. | 8: 31-35. 8: 38. 9: 1. | | |
| XXIX..205. | The Transfiguration | Mt. Hermon | 17: 1, 5-7. 17: 9-13. | 9: 3, 6, 8. 9: 10-12. | 9: 28-35. | |
| XXIX..209. | The Epileptic Cured | Casarea Philippi | 17: 15. 17: 18-20. | 9: 14-16. 9: 20-27, 29. | 9: 37-41. 9: 43- | |
| XXX..210. | Journey through Galilee | Galilee | 17: 22-23. | 9: 30-32. | 9: 43-45. 9: 48. | |
| XXX..213. | The Tribute Money | Capernaum | 17: 24-27. 18: 3-5, 7. 18: 10-35. | 9: 33-36. 9: 38-50. | 19: 10. | |
| XXXI..217. | The Sending of the Seventy | Perea | | | 10: 1-24. | 7: 1. |
| XXXI..221. | Steadfastly Goes to Jerusalem | | | | 9: 51-56. | 7: 2-9. |
| XXXII..225. | The Ten Lepers | Border of Samaria and Galilee | | | 17: 12-19. | |
| XXXII..226. | The Good Samaritan | Perea | | | 10: 25-37. | |
| XXXII..229. | The Lord's Prayer | | | | 11: 1-13. | 7: 11-52. |
| XXXIII..237. | The Woman Taken in Adultery | Jerusalem | | | 10: 38-42. | 7: 53-8: 11. |
| XXXIV..238. | The True Children of God | " | | | | 8: 12-59. |

| CHAP. P. | EVENTS. | PLACE. | MATT. | MARK. | LUKE. | JOHN. |
|---|---|---|---|---|---|---|
| XXXV..246. | The Blind Man and the Pharisees | Jerusalem | | | | 9: 1-41. |
| XXXVI..253. | Christ the Good Shepherd | | | | | 10: 1-42. |
| XXXVII..258. | The Law of Divorce | Perea | 19: 10-12. | 10: 2-12. | | |
| XXXVII..261. | Little Children | | | 10: 13-16. | | |
| XXXVII..261. | Riches a Snare | | 19: 17-22. | 10: 17, 18, 21. | | |
| | | | 19: 27-20: 16. | 10: 23-27. | | |
| XXXVIII..265. | The Sabbath and Good Works | " | | | 13: 10-21. | |
| | | | | | 13: 23-35. | |
| XXXVIII..270. | The Sabbath and the Pharisees | | | | 14: 1-6. | |
| XXXVIII..270. | The Chief Seats | | | | 14: 7-24. | |
| XXXIX..274. | The Cross to be Borne | | | | 14: 25-15: 2. | |
| XXXIX..277. | The Lost Sheep | Perea | | | 15: 3-10. | |
| XXXIX..277. | The Prodigal Son | | | | 15: 11-32. | |
| XL..281. | The Unjust Steward | " | | | 16: 1-18. | |
| XL..285. | The Rich Man and Lazarus | " | | | 16: 19-17: 10. | |
| XLI..289. | The Kingdom of God within | Between Samaria and Galilee | | | 17: 20-37. | |
| XLI..290. | The Unjust Judge | Between Samaria and Galilee | | | 18: 1-8. | |
| XLI..290. | Self-righteousness | Between Samaria and Galilee | | | 18: 9-14. | |
| XLIII..293. | Lazarus | Bethany | | | 18: 34. | 11: 1-54. |
| XLIII..301. | Jesus Predicts His Death | Perea | | 10: 32-34. | | |
| XLIII..301. | The Sons of Zebedee | | 20: 20-28. | | | |
| XLIII..302. | The Blind Bartimæus | Jericho | | 10: 46-51. | 18: 42-43. | |
| XLIII..305. | Zacchæus | " | | | 19: 1-10. | |
| XLIII..305. | The Misused Talent | " | | | 19: 11-28. | |
| XLIV..309. | | | | | | 11: 55-57. |

| Chap. P. | Events | Places | Matt. | Mark. | Luke. | John. |
|---|---|---|---|---|---|---|
| LII..366. | Judas | Jerusalem | 26: 22-25. | 14: 22-24. | 22: 21, 23. | 13: 21-38. |
| | | | 26: 27-29. | | | 14: 1-31. |
| LIII..370. | The Farewell | " | | | | 15: 1-27. |
| LIV..374. | The Farewell | " | | | | 16: 1-33. |
| LV..378. | The Farewell | " | | | | 17: 1-26. |
| LVI..385. | Jesus' Last Prayer | | 26: 30-33. | 14: 30-32. | 22: 31-33. | 18: 1. |
| LVII..389. | Satan Sifting Peter | | 26: 36. | | | 18: 1, 2. |
| LVII..389. | | | | | 22: 35-38, 40. | |
| LVII..390. | The Agony | Gethsemane | 26: 37-39. | 14: 36-44. | 22: 43-46. | 18: 4-12. |
| | | | 26: 49, 50. | | 22: 48, 49. | |
| | | | 26: 52-56. | 14: 50-52. | 22: 51, 53. | |
| | | | 26: 42, 44. | 14: 53. | | |
| LVII..397. | Trial Before Annas | Jerusalem | | | | 18: 13. |
| | | | | | | 18: 19-24. |
| LVIII..398. | Trial Before Caiaphas | " | 26: 59, 60. | 14: 57-62. | 22: 63-65. | 18: 14-16. |
| | | | 26: 63, 65. | 14: 64, 65. | | 18: 18. |
| LVIII..401. | Peter's Remorse | " | 26: 71, 73. | 14: 66-68. | 22: 61. | 18: 26. |
| | | | 26: 74, 75. | 14: 70. | | |
| LIX..402. | Trial Before Sanhedrin | " | 27: 2-10. | 15: 1. | 22: 66-71. | |
| LIX..405. | Trials Before Pilate and Herod | " | 27: 11, 15-17. | 15: 7, 8, 10. | 23: 2, 5-16. | 18: 28-38. |
| | | | 27: 19, 20. | 15: 12, 15-20. | 23: 18, 20. | 19: 4-16. |
| | | | 27: 22-25. | | 23: 22, 23, 25. | |
| LX..414. | The Crucifixion | Calvary | 27: 36, 39-43. | 15: 21, 25. | 23: 26-37. | 19: 17, 18. |
| | | | 27: 51-54. | 15: 33-36. | 23: 39-43. | 19: 19-37. |
| | | | | 15: 40, 41. | 23: 46-48. | |
| LXI..422. | The Burial | Garden near Calvary | 27: 57, 60. | 15: 44-46. | 23: 50, 51. | 19: 38-42. |
| | | | 27: 61. | | 23: 55, 56. | |
| LXI..425. | The Resurrection | Garden near Calvary | 27: 62-66. | 16: 1-8. | 24: 4-9. | 20: 2. |
| | | | 28: 1-4, 7. | | | 20: 2-18. |
| | | | 28: 8, 11-15. | | 24: 12. | |
| LXII..429. | | | | | | |

| C. r. P. | Events. | Place. | Matt. | Mark. | Luke. | John. |
|---|---|---|---|---|---|---|
| LXIII..433. | Appearances... | ............ | 28: 8-10. | 16: 9-12. | 24: 10, 11. | 20: 19. |
|  |  |  | ............ | 16: 14-18. | 24: 13-18. | 20: 21-29. |
| LXIV..441. | Appearances... | ............ | ............ | I. Cor. | ............ | 22: 1-24. |
| LXV..446. | Appearances... | ............ | 28: 16-20. | 15: 6, 7. | 24: 49. | ............ |
|  |  |  | ............ | Mark. | Acts 1: 3-8. | Acts |
| LXV..449. | The Ascension... | Mt. of Olives. | ............ | 16: 20. | Luke. | 1: 9-11. |
|  |  |  | ............ | ............ | 24: 50-53. | 6: 7. |

www.ingramcontent.com/pod-product-compliance
Lightning Source LLC
Chambersburg PA
CBHW022019110726
47901CB00006B/1585